Ibrahim

THE LAST
PROSPECTING
GUIDE

You'll Ever
NEED

— DIRECT SALES EDITION —

THE LAST
PROSPECTING
GUIDE

YOU'LL EVER
NEED

DIRECT SALES EDITION

BOB BURG

CO-AUTHOR OF THE INTERNATIONAL
BEST SELLER "THE GO-GIVER"

Sound Wisdom
167 Walnut Bottom Road
Shippensburg, PA 17257

www.soundwisdom.com

Tremendous Life Books
206 W. Allen Street
Mechanicsburg, PA 17055
www.tremendouselifebooks.com

This book and all other Sound Wisdom books are available at bookstores and distributors worldwide.

ISBN 13:978-1-937879-12-9
ISBN Ebook:978-1-937879-13-6

For Worldwide Distribution, Printed in the U.S.A.

3 4 5 6 7 / 16 15 14 13

TABLE OF CONTENTS

PREFACE

Okay, there's good news and bad news.

Here's the good news. You truly have your hands on the best business opportunity on the face of the Earth. You are in the exact right place to build your business, and at the exact right time. Your line of mentorship is the best, the business-building system you get to learn from is tops, and the company behind your business is beyond reproach, with years of experience and success.

The industry itself?

Network Marketing/Direct Selling has created millionaires and has been a vehicle for financial and time freedom for free-enterprising individuals just like you for so many years that its viability is now considered to be self-evident. Top magazines have featured Network Marketing/Direct Selling, giving it respect and credibility. And you've got the tools and resources to help you succeed. Companies have invested millions upon millions of dollars in the latest technological trends and equipment, and media such as teleconferences and videoconferences abound. You're part of an infrastructure that puts you in the driver's seat on the highway of life.

That's the good news. And you'll agree; it's pretty darn good!

So, what's the bad news?

Well, actually, it's not really even bad news. More like, "real-world" news. And that is simply the following; even though you are affiliated with a truly wonderful company, with the greatest products in the business, and with the potential to make a tremendous amount of money and enjoy a lifestyle of comfort and freedom . . . THIS IS A PEOPLE BUSINESS!!!!! It always has been, is now, and always will be.

So, Bob, it's a people business. Big deal. Why is that bad news? Oh, I'm sorry; I mean "real-world" news? What I mean is, why are you making a big deal about the fact that it's a people business? Of course it is.

People can be difficult. There . . . I said it. Quite frankly, it's no big surprise to you is it? Difficult and not always logical. Presented with a chance to break out of mediocrity, reclaim their lives, provide better for their families, give more to the charitable causes in which they believe, and live the American Dream, most people will "just say no." Now, I believe in just saying "no" when it comes to certain things. But why would anyone say "no" to you, your products, your company, and your opportunity?

Here's the answer: I don't know.

Now for the REALLY good news . . . **it doesn't matter.** That's because there are enough people out there who are looking for this exact opportunity, that all you have to do is be prepared for, and not be discouraged by, the "no's." Keep going through enough "no's" so that you will eventually find the "yesses." And it doesn't matter how many prospects say no. It doesn't matter because you know:

> **There's an endless number of people out there who you can confidently approach with ease in a way that you won't have to feel nervous or uptight, and they'll be totally open to the idea of being approached by you regarding a business opportunity.**

But Bob, unfortunately, I'm not a "networking professional." I don't know an endless number of people that I can confidently approach.

I understand. Please don't feel you're alone. Countless others have felt exactly the same way. Then, they discovered there was a prospecting method; a *system* they could use that would allow them to put as many people in front of their business plan as they desired. And with this system in place, they never, ever again had to ask themselves that most dreaded of questions:

"Who do I talk to next, now that my original list of names has run out?"

The information in this booklet will take you, step-by step, on a journey toward that never-ending list of new, high-quality prospects. It's like a map that will lead you to buried treasure!

Before we move on to Chapter One, I must make three statements:

1. This system absolutely works, and has been used with great success by distributors, consultants,

independent business owners, salespeople and associates affiliated with many different companies.

2. Luck has nothing to do with it; it is strictly a matter of cause and effect. Do the right things and you'll get the right results.

3. If it seems like I'm bragging, I'm not. I take absolutely no credit for these methods, techniques, success principles, etc. I've learned far more from others than I've ever taught. In fact, I can genuinely say, "I've never had an original thought in my life!" I am very grateful to all those from whom I've learned, and honored to be able to share this with you. Don't be afraid to share them with others – as you'll see, there's no shortage of prospects, so there's no reason to keep these prospecting methods secret!

I wish you the best of success as you help lots of people change their lives for the better.

TO YOU AND YOUR FREEDOM!

Bob Burg

CHAPTER 1

THE MINDSET

(Your Only Inventory Is People)

You began with a healthy list of names. People you knew. Family, friends, lots of acquaintances. You were excited. You were fired up. And you knew (and you *knew* that you knew) that all those people on your list would be just as excited about this incredible opportunity as you were. How could they possibly not be?

You made some calls and got some "no's." Approached people personally and got some more "no's." Handed out some really cool, high-tech informational materials and continued to get "no's." Went back to calling on the phone and received even more "no's." It may have even begun to remind you of that hit song from the early 70's that went something like, "No no no, no no nononono, no nono, nono no no, no no nononono . . ."

And you began to wonder. . .

Uh-oh. What a lousy feeling. What's going on? Why aren't these people interested? Are they nuts? What is it they're not interested in? Financial freedom? A less-stressful lifestyle? The life-changing products?

Let's back up just a bit, to the very first words uttered in the previous paragraph. They were, "Uh-oh."

Uh-oh, meaning, "Uh-oh, if many more people continue to tell me 'no' I'm going to sooner or later (most likely sooner) run out of names of people to call. Then what will I do? I'll be out of business!"

Now, we know how important it is to keep exposing the business to people, right? After all, the mega-successes always teach, "He or she who shows the business the most, wins." In other words, it doesn't really matter how many people say "no" as long as you find enough people who say "yes."

THE SECRET OF CHAMPIONS

At the time of this writing, I've been privileged to have spoken at over 90 different Direct Selling and Network Marketing organizations. When I started, I'd ask the top producers, "What is it that has made you so successful in the business?" They'd talk about the system of books, audios, seminars, conventions, voice-mail, three-way-calls, etc. Then I'd ask, "Well, a lot of people do that, and with great success. I mean, many of them are obviously on the fast track, but they're not there yet, so what is the *determining* factor . . . the reason why you are at the top level while they are not?"

Their answer was *always – now get this -* always *the same*: "Those of us who've reached the top level of the company have simply shared the business with more people than those who are not yet there." In other words, it doesn't really matter how many people say "no," as long as you find enough people who say "yes."

Could that really be it? But that's so simple.

Ah, yes *Grasshopper* (remember the old Kung Fu television show?), *simple*, but not necessarily *easy*.

You might be asking yourself:

How do I find all those people to talk to? Because the way things are going right now, my list of names is running out fast and furious. I've approached almost everyone I know, even people I don't know that well. And I'm starting to get the feeling that people are avoiding me. Maybe Network Marketing just isn't for me.

So how do you find all those new people to talk to? That's exactly what we're going to address.

By the way, about those rejections - that was bad enough, but wasn't the worst part the fact that you could sense you were beginning to sound needy, if not downright desperate? As though you needed them more than they needed you? Actually, you would even have settled for someone just to affirm you were doing the right thing. But people are interesting, aren't they? If they sense desperation, they are less inclined to be interested. And that was definitely happening.

POSTURE

That's where a concept called "posture" comes in. I define posture as "when you care ... but not *that* much!" What's interesting about posture is that the more of it you have, the more people will respond to you in a positive manner. When they sense you don't care that much whether they are interested, they suddenly become more interested. "Hmm, what is she doing that's so great that she doesn't really care that I'm not interested?" And even if they don't say "yes," posture gives you more confidence as you move on to your next prospect.

I don't just mean acting like you don't care that much. True posture, the kind that works, is when you *really don't* care that much!

Please don't get me wrong. Yes, you care about the person, but you are in no way "attached" to the results of your conversation. Network marketing super-achievers are great at that, aren't they? If someone isn't interested, they don't dwell on it, and they certainly don't take it personally. They just move on down the road and get back to work. They are experts at saying "N-E-X-T!"

As far as I can tell, there are only two ways to develop true posture. One way is to have such faith in yourself as an unstoppable business-builder combined with a belief that G-d is ultimately calling the shots anyway, that you work with the realization that as long as you control your activity, G-d will control the results. It's easy to have true posture with that attitude.

The other way is to continually develop and have such a huge and ever-growing list of quality names that you know you can never possibly run out of prospects. That will also provide you with true posture.

Ideally, you'll have both of the above – faith and a never-ending list of prospects!

Let's begin talking about the second way right now. I'll leave the first way up to you and your mentors.

KNOW YOU, LIKE YOU, TRUST YOU

Let's begin with what I call the "Golden Rule" of Business Networking:

> **All things being equal, people will do business with, and refer business to, those people they know, like and trust.**

Think about it; isn't that how you are as a consumer? Other than what you can buy through your own business, isn't it true that when you shop for a car, furniture, clothes, or anything else, if the price, service, and all other determining factors are equal (or even close to equal), don't you buy from – and refer others to – those salespeople you know, like and trust? Business is all about relationships.

And you probably refer others to them as well, with pleasure, don't you?

It's the same with your business, whether we're talking about your customers, or people you want to have as part of your team. Of course, for the purpose of this book, we're talking about building an organization, and will proceed with that in mind.

Your job is to now take on the mindset of developing relationships with people, and cultivating these relationships to the point where the new people you meet, on a daily basis, feel good about you. They feel so good about you, that they feel as though they know you, they like you, and they trust you (and for good reason – you are the type of person who deserves those feelings toward you in another person). They want to see you succeed, they want to help you find new business, possibly they want to be a part of your business; they definitely want to be a part of your life.

And we'll talk about how to bring about those feelings in a quick and timely manner. More importantly, we'll discuss specifically how to accomplish this in a way that makes the process of prospecting relaxing, comfortable and fun. That's right – fun! No more stomach tension because you need to go out doing something you don't want to do. No more defensiveness as you approach someone who doesn't want to be approached, to talk about something they don't want to talk about. This system will indeed make prospecting downright fun!

The Law of 250

Joe Girard was a car salesperson based in Detroit, Michigan. "So what?" you might ask, "What does that have to do with me?" Well, the car sales part maybe nothing. But the wisdom he imparts, plenty. You see, Joe Girard, for 14 years in a row was listed in the Guinness Book of World Records as the most successful car salesperson in the world in terms of numbers sold. You've learned through the success system you plug into through your line of mentorship that wisdom in one area of life typically applies across the board, and can be applied to your business as well, correct? Well, you and I probably both believe that anyone who has been that successful for such a consistently long time probably has some wisdom to impart to us that we can successfully employ. So, what is that wisdom?

In his bestselling book, *How to Sell Anything to Anybody* (no, I don't like the title either, but the book itself is excellent), Joe explains what he calls Girard's Law of 250. This Law simply says that each of us has a personal sphere of influence (those we know naturally, i.e., close family, distant relatives, close friends, acquaintances, those we went to school with, work with, our plumber, tailor, barber/hairstylist, our accountant, lawyer, etc.)

of about 250 people. According to Girard, that's how many people will attend our wedding . . . and our funeral!

Even if his numbers for those two major events seem somewhat high, the 250 figure still works out. For instance, if you were to take a pencil and paper and write down the names of everybody you know (and I mean everybody!), using the memory-jogging information you received when you first joined your company, you would have a list of about 250 people.

Try this little exercise: grab the Yellow Pages phonebook (or go to www.allpages.com) and browse through the business classifications, beginning with "A" and ending with "Z." How many people can you identify? Who do you know who is a (an):

A. Accountant, Ad Rep, Attorney, etc.

B. Baker, Banker, Builder, etc.

C. Chiropractor, Cleaning Company Owner, Computer Software Professional, etc.

Back to this in a moment.

Please understand that when you recruit or sponsor a new member of your team and they write down only three names ("That's everyone I know" – even though they have five siblings), that isn't truly their entire sphere of influence. They are really communicating that, based on their lack of knowledge about the business and lack of self-confidence (at this time), that's all the names they are willing to risk sharing with you right now.

That's okay, as long as you understand that. Then you are in a position to assure them that even though you are going to help them come up with 250 names right now, you and they will only begin contacting those people once they feel ready to do so.

Okay, now let's address that 250-person center of influence that everyone has. What's not important is that *you* know 250 people. What is key is the fact that <u>every new person you meet *also* knows 250 people</u>.

That's right; every time you establish and cultivate a relationship with one new person, and develop that relationship to the point that that person feels as though he knows you, likes you, and trusts you, you have increased your personal sphere of influence by 250 people . . . EVERY SINGLE TIME! Develop a relationship with just one new person a day, and in practically no time at all, you will have an absolutely enormous, humongous personal sphere of influence!

This simple but powerful concept is certainly one key to huge success in Network Marketing – and it can be the key to your personal success as well.

HOW TO FIND THEM, MEET THEM, AND WIN THEM OVER

The only question left is how to do it. The theory is simple enough – but how do you actually put yourself in a position to add people to your names list – your inventory – on a continual basis, every day, 250 people at a time?

First we must ask, "where can we find good prospects?" The answer is "practically everywhere." The next question is, "where can we find these people in a setting that lends itself to approaching them in a very laid-back, non-threatening manner (and this is important . . . non-threatening to them, and you!). Only then is there an opportunity to meet them, and begin the process of establishing a mutually beneficial, win/win relationship.

In the next chapter, you'll learn how to accomplish this, and build your inventory to an enormous level.

CHAPTER 2

THE PROCESS

(10 Steps to Cultivating Prospects from Thin Air)

There's a good reason why the situations/places/events in which you meet quality potential prospects must be conducive to your approaching them. A reason why both you and the other person need to feel non-threatened, and even good about the process. Of course, it's pretty obvious why the prospect must feel this way.

The reason why it is so vitally important for <u>you</u> to feel this way is that you need to see the prospecting process as being fun. It can be. But it's only fun when the nervousness (sick, nauseated feeling in the gut) typically associated with prospecting is no longer there. And this only happens when the situation for meeting someone you wish to prospect allows for a natural feeling of comfort. Don't worry; those situations abound! It will never again be a problem for you.

Places and Faces

So where do these positive prospecting situations occur? Let's list just a few places. One would be a social/business event such as a monthly Chamber of Commerce "Business After Hours" event. Although these gatherings are typically worthless for most people – and you may have experienced that same result – they can be pure, solid gold for you. It's only a matter of approaching these events, and working them, the correct way.

Another great place to prospect is a purely social gathering, such as a party. And the more people you *don't* know, the merrier. Don't get nervous here; the prospecting process will be a breeze! I'm just wanting to help you find situations in which there are people you don't know, because, those are the new people to add to your growing *inventory*.

Still another wonderful place to meet quality prospects is at local charity events. Why? Because (besides the fact that just your being there means you are supporting a charity) charity events attract two types of people – those who already are successful (those are the type who *get* this business the quickest, right?) and those who are on their way to being successful. I'm sure you're willing to help both types accomplish their goals, aren't you?

The megabookstore/coffee shop is an awesome place to meet prospects of high quality. Leaders are readers, and readers are often potential leaders. Many of them will begin to read a book while enjoying a delicious, relaxing latte.

But Bob, approaching a stranger who is reading and drinking a cup of coffee is exactly what I don't want to do!

Don't worry. We are not near that point yet. When it's time, it'll be a piece of cake.

And plenty of other opportunities to meet great new people on a daily business will take place as well. As you become more comfortable with the prospecting process and discover how fun it truly is, your antennae will go up and situations you never recognized before (possibly because you didn't want to) will regularly appear in your life. Ball games, PTA meetings, the health club, you name it. Again, these situations are not new; only the way you will see them and handle them.

BEGIN THE PROCESS

Let's begin by pretending you are in, what would seem to many people, the worst situation for prospecting they could possibly be in. You've just joined your local Chamber of Commerce and they are having a big "Business After Hours" event with well over 100 people attending. At this point, you know absolutely nobody there. Bad or good? Good . . . very good!

But Bob. . . you still don't understand! I'm not like my upline leaders. I mean, I'm not smooth. I can't just walk into a place where I don't know anyone and start talking to people.

Good, then you are like I am. Because nothing would scare me more than to think I have to approach a bunch of strangers and begin talking to them about my business.

So let's back up a moment and, before we meet anyone, systemize this process.

Step Number One: Adjust your attitude to the understanding that the reason you are attending this event is to work. To build your names list. To increase your inventory. That doesn't mean you won't have fun. In fact, this type of prospecting is some of the most fun you will ever have. But you are there to work.

Step Number Two: Prepare to "work the room." How? Simply recognize the "lay of the land," so to speak. Where are people standing and/or sitting? Where is the hors d'oeuvre table? Where is the refreshments table? Where are the restrooms? Notice the people gathered in groups of four, five or six people who are conversing and relating to each other. Take a walk around the room and experience its "feel."

Step Number Three: Locate – don't approach, just locate – several "centers of influence." What do I mean by that term? Remember earlier we spoke about your sphere of influence – the people you know? Well, centers of influence are those people who already have a very large, powerful, even prestigious sphere of influence. They've been around for a while now and know a lot of people. People who know them, like them and trust them.

These centers of influence are the people you want to make a point of meeting at this event. Making personal connections with just two or three of them – that eventually turn into connections of the "know, like and trust" variety - will give you access to lots of other quality prospects, each with their *own* 250-person sphere of influence.

But how do you know who these centers of influence are if you don't know any of the people at the event? My good friend and prospecting mentor, Rick Hill, taught me a wonderful method to quickly and efficiently determine this. Just casually notice the interactions of the small groups and you'll quickly notice that one person in each group is sort of the unofficial group leader.

This is the person around whom the conversation sort of evolves. In other words, when they laugh, the rest of the group laughs. When they give a disgusted look at something someone says, all the others do the same. Nine times out of ten, this person is a center of influence, and well worth getting to know one-on-one. With this in mind, let's move on to . . .

Step Number Four: Meet one of these centers of influence one-on-one.

But how do you do that, if they are involved in a group discussion? After all, besides the fact that breaking into someone else's (who you don't yet know) conversation is somewhat rude and will generally not accomplish what you want – good feelings toward you in the other person – it is also very awkward and scary. So again, please don't put that kind of pressure on yourself. It is totally unnecessary.

So what should you do? Just wait patiently for one of the several centers of influence you've picked out of the crowd to leave their present group. Sooner or later, one of them will. Why? For a variety of reasons. Possibly to get something to eat or drink, use the restroom, move on to another group, meet new people with whom to network for their own business, and who knows why else? But eventually, they will move on. When that happens, be ready.

For example, let's say one of them, a young 30-something gentleman walks towards the hors d'oeuvres table. Well, head on over there as well. Stay calm, and have a genuine, warm smile on your face. Gently make eye contact with him. When he sees you, just smile and say hello. Most likely, he'll do the same.

If he doesn't, that's fine. Maybe he's got something else on his mind. Perhaps he's supposed to meet someone and he doesn't want to get involved in another conversation right now. Or, he wants to take a moment to think about a personal challenge he needs to deal with.

For whatever reason, the timing might not be right at this point to meet him. Or possibly he's just an unfriendly person. Who knows; who cares? If you're supposed to one day meet this particular person, you will. If not, you won't. No problem either way. Just say to yourself, "NEXT" and wait for another center of influence to leave their group.

Now let me share something with you. The chances are greater than 99 out of 100 that this person will in fact smile right back at you and say "hello." When he does, just extend your hand and introduce yourself. He will do the same. Now just ask him what line of work he is in. He'll gladly tell you, and ask you the same. Briefly mention your "J.O.B." (what you do for a living until you're ready to go full-time in your Network Marketing business) or respond along the lines of "I'm a business development consultant" or another brief, generic statement that applies to your business.

But please keep this in mind, as this is key; here is where you . . . **DON'T TALK ABOUT YOUR COMPANY OR YOUR PRODUCTS!!!!!** Now is not the time!

YOUR INITIAL CONVERSATION

The only thing you are going to talk about right now is him. Not because you have anything to hide. Not one bit. It's just that he doesn't care about you and your business (and please understand this - *yet*). He cares about himself and his business.

Step Number Five: Begin rapport-building. This is accomplished by letting him do practically all of the talking. And you do practically all of the listening. This is powerful for two reasons; one is that it is totally stress-free (there's no pressure on you to be witty, quick, clever, etc.). The other is that it's very effective at developing his good feelings towards you.

Hey, isn't it true that the people we find most interesting are the people who seem most interested . . . in us? How many times have you been in a conversation with someone who let you do practically all of the talking, and then afterwards said to yourself, "Wow, what a fascinating conversationalist!" And you felt really good about them. It's happened to me, and I know this system!

Step Number Six: Ask several open-ended, *Feel-good Questions*™. Open-ended questions are simply questions that you cannot answer with a simple yes or no, but require a longer response. Open-ended questions usually (but not always) begin with "Who, what, when, where, why, and how."

The most important part to this step however, is the feel-good part. A *Feel-good Question*™ is a question that, by its very nature, results in your prospect feeling good about himself, about the conversation, and about you! This part of the prospecting process is the key to unlocking the door to the relationship. And the nicest part about it is that you can sort of sit back and let your prospect be the star.

Asking questions designed to make your prospect feel good about himself or herself sort of flies in the face of some of the more traditional methods of prospecting. How many times have we heard, "Find that person's pain" or "Get them to admit they are in a rut?" Of course, at times (such as, in the actual presentation process) this might be appropriate, but now is definitely not the time. The "know you, like you, trust you" relationship has not yet been established.

Instead of finding your prospect's pain, find his joy. Keep in mind that everybody wears an invisible sign around his or her neck that says, "Please, make me feel important. Make me feel good about myself."

People gravitate to those who make them feel better when in their presence then when not. Isn't that how you feel around your leaders? One of my favorite Talmudic expressions is, "Who is honored? One who honors others." Honor your prospects (and everyone else in your life) by making them feel good about themselves.

So what are some of these *Feel-good Questions*™?

I have five *Feel-good Questions*™ I'd like to share with you. Please understand, however, that you won't ever have time to ask all of them. You'll only have time to ask a couple of them. And the first two are probably the best. Asking only these two questions will make a significant difference in your effectiveness with your prospects. Nonetheless, let's review all five so you'll have them at your disposal whenever you feel you might need them.

The Actual Questions

Feel-good Question™ #1: *"How did you get started in the 'widget' business?"*

I call this the "Movie-of-the-Week" question because most people love the opportunity to "tell their story" to someone. Inevitably, people are delighted that someone actually wants to know about them, instead of just talking about themselves. And they are doubly impressed by the fact that they just met you, and you're asking about them. Be sure and actively listen, and be interested in what they are saying.

Feel-good Question™ #2: *"What do you enjoy most about what you do?"*

Again, you are giving them something very positive to associate with you and your conversation. It's a positive question which elicits a positive response, and good feelings. This is much better than asking the alternative question, "So, tell me about the awful job you have . . . as well as this wretched excuse for a life you live." (Only kidding, but you get the point.)

Feel-good Question™ #3: *"What separates your company from the competition?"*

I call this the "permission-to-brag" question. All our lives we're taught not to brag about ourselves and our accomplishments, yet you've just given this person carte blanche to let it all hang out. With every syllable this person says, the feelings he associates with you become stronger and more positive.

Feel-good Question™ #4: *"What advice would you give someone just starting out in your line of work?"*

This is what I call my "mentor" question. Don't we all like to feel as though others would benefit from our knowledge and experience? Provide your prospect an opportunity to feel like a mentor by asking this question.

Feel-good Question™ #5: *"What's the most memorable (or funniest) incident you've ever experienced in your business?"*

This is my "war story" question. Bring back the good times with this one, or even those moments that, even if they weren't too funny at the time, can't help but make your prospect smile now. People enjoy telling war stories, and this question provides them with an opportunity to do so.

Bonus Feel-good Question™: *"What do you forecast as the coming trends in your industry?"*

This question works very well with the types who really want to share with you their knowledge of their industry. Even those who might not really know a whole lot. A "Cliff Claven" type (remember him from the television show, Cheers?) will love you as soon as you ask him or her this question.

The One "Key" Question That Will Set You Apart From Everyone Else Your Prospect Has Ever Met

Yes, I realize that's a very strong statement, but it's really true. Not only have I noticed that in my own life when asking people this question, but the strongest letters I receive from those who read my books, listen to my audio programs, or attend my live presentations have to do with this question, and the accompanying results. It really works, and you'll see why. First, know that this question is only to be asked once the initial rapport has been established. Here it is:

"How can I know if someone I'm speaking to would be a good prospect for you?"

What have you done by asking that question? The answer is twofold. First, you've continued to separate yourself from the "average" person and affirmed to your prospect that you are interested in him, as opposed to just you. Most people are "I" oriented; they think only of themselves, and it is quite obvious to the prospect. You, on the other hand, are "you" oriented;

you're thinking of your prospect and his needs. That is <u>very much</u> appreciated.

Secondly, you have just given your prospect an opportunity to actually tell you how to help them find new business! Imagine that. No one has ever done that for him before. Most likely, his own loved ones have never done that before. But you have. And he'll have an answer for you. Most likely, an answer you would never expect to hear.

For example, let's pretend your prospect's name is Gary. Gary sells copying machines locally for one of the major copying machine manufacturers. He knows ways to spot a good prospect for his product that most of us are not aware of. Thus, when you ask, "Gary, how can I know if someone I'm speaking to would be a good prospect for you?" he'll have an answer.

In fact, after thinking about it for just a quick moment, he responds, "Well, if you ever happen to be walking in an office and you notice a copying machine . . . and next to that copying machine is a wastepaper basket which is filled to the very rim with crumpled up pieces of paper, that's a really good sign that copying machine has been breaking down a lot lately . . . and that would be an excellent prospect for me!"

So Gary has just told you how to help him; how to network for him. And, more than anything, he appreciates the very fact that you asked. He is very quickly developing very positive feelings towards you. He knows that you are in fact a person with whom it would be very well worth developing a relationship.

By the way, you might be wondering, "What if I'm in a conversation with a person who's not in sales and doesn't have, prospects, per se?" That's fine. The basic principles still apply. If this person is a company CEO or in the accounting department, thus wouldn't necessarily be looking for prospects, you can still ask any of the *Feel-good Questions™* we just discussed.

Now, however, the One "Key" Question, instead of being, "How can I know if someone I'm speaking to would be a good prospect for you?" might be, "How can I know if someone I'm speaking with is someone you'd like to meet?" or be, "How can I know if someone I'm speaking to could be of benefit to you in some way?"

Again, since this methodology is "Principle-based" you can veer slightly from the "tactics" without losing its essence.

A networker by the name of "Mary" was talking to a person named "Bill," an upper-management type for a traditional corporation and a true center of influence. During the conversation she discovered that his daughter, Jill, had just graduated from college and was looking for a job in a certain field. Her One "Key" Question to Bill became, "How can I know if someone I'm speaking to would be a good contact for Jill?"

According to Mary, "You should have seen Bill's eyes light right up. He was amazed that someone he just met would take such an interest in his daughter instead of just trying to sell him on their own product or service."

Of course, Mary, being the great networker she is, didn't leave it at that. Once Bill told her, she went out and actively found someone, and introduced that person directly to Bill. Bill put that person together with his daughter, who wound up getting, not only some great advice, but a job! Do you think Bill was appreciative of Mary? You bet.

By the way, Bill never did join Mary's business but he sure was a wonderful source of referrals. Is there any wonder why?

Another type of question you can ask is called FORM questions. "FORM" (or, F-O-R-M) is an acronym that stands for Family, Occupation, Recreation and Message.

F is for Family. Ask your prospect about his or her family. Do people enjoy talking about their family? Usually, they sure do. Their talented spouse, or their straight A-achieving or athletic child. Encourage them to talk about those they love, and they'll love you for it.

O is for Occupation. We've already discussed that. Even if they're not in sales, per se, you can still ask the (feel good questions.) But, the one key question might be, "How can I know if someone I am talking to is someone you'd like to meet?"

R is for Recreation. People love talking about their recreational activities, don't they? Does he or she ski, play tennis, bowl, mountain climb or something else? People are generally very excited and passionate about their recreation. You can easily ask them how they got started, what they enjoy most about it, and what advice they'd have for others in this area.

M is for Message. What is it they value? Are they involved with a charitable, religious or political activity? "But wait, don't they say to never discuss religion or politics?" Oh, I don't know about that. You can discuss it...just don't argue about it. Be supportive.

CONCLUDE AND MOVE ON

Step Number Seven: End your conversation with Gary. It's time for you to meet another center of influence, and begin another potentially great mutually beneficial relationship. Before leaving Gary however, make sure you ask him for his business card. Only offer yours after he asks for it, and realize that your card will probably be thrown out as soon as he gets home (along with the dozens of others he received at this event).

Even if your business card isn't thrown out, it will, at best, be relegated to his Rolodex®. Maybe even his computer's contact management system . . . which he probably doesn't use more than an extremely limited amount. That's okay; that's just the way it is. What's important is that you received *his* business card. More on that in the next chapter.

Step Number Eight: Introduce yourself to your next prospect. Maybe another of the several centers of influence you noticed earlier. Or even someone else who happens to be where you are standing. Naturally, you don't want to limit yourself to just talking to certain people. After all, you never know if today's non-center of influence is tomorrow's mover-and-shaker. And sometimes, that person who doesn't seem to crave the spotlight is simply a very humble, ultra-successful person.

The method for picking out centers of influence is simply a guide to help you. Don't feel as though you need to limit yourself regarding who you talk to. And, one more thing; if you see a person who looks genuinely shy and bashful and as though they could use a friendly person to speak to, go out of your way to meet them. It's just a nice thing to do. And, interestingly enough, it'll never come back to haunt you. Usually, it's just the opposite.

So, what do you do when meeting your next prospect? Well . . . nothing any different then you did with your last prospect. You smile, introduce yourself, and invest 99.9 percent of the conversation asking her about herself and her business. You do this via *Feel-good Questions*™. And then you ask her the one key question, "How can I know if someone I'm talking to would be a good prospect for you?" Get her card and finish up the conversation, letting her know how much you enjoyed meeting her. Then take your leave and introduce yourself to another person – remember, there are always plenty of people at these events who would love to meet someone like yourself who is genuinely interested in them! Sounds pretty simple, right? Just remember to have fun with this, and not put any undue pressure on yourself. You don't need to be perfect. Just keep doing this, and build on your small successes. You'll be amazed by your results, almost immediately!

By the way, the process of meeting a person and the questions you ask, work regardless of whether it takes place at an organized event such as the one we are now imagining, or meeting in a one-on-one situation anywhere else. Later, we'll talk about how to meet people in various "non-organized event" situations. And if that was the case, there wouldn't be anything left for you to do regarding your initial conversation. Since we are at an actual event, however, you can still add to the impressions you have made thus far.

CONTINUE TO MAKE A GREAT IMPRESSION

Step Number Nine: Remember your prospect's name. It's 45 minutes later. You've met three, four or five good prospects, and are now standing by the hors d'oeuvres table, having a quick, enjoyable bite. Gary, the copying machine salesperson you met earlier, walks over to grab a snack. As you spot him, call him by name. "Hey Gary, good to see you again."

He'll most likely be amazed and delighted because, by this time, he has probably forgotten your name. Nothing personal, and since we've all done that, it doesn't surprise us. But in remembering his name, you'll have again made a huge impact on him. (There are good, inexpensive books you can purchase on how to remember names, but the key in this case is that you haven't tried to focus on everyone; just a few people. Every so often, throughout the event, glance at the people you've met to remind yourself of their names.)

Key point: reintroduce yourself to him by name, so that he doesn't feel defensive and/or embarrassed by the fact he didn't remember your name. So Networker Steve might say, "Hi Gary, Steve Johnson. We met a bit earlier, nice to see you again. Great food, isn't it?" Now you've totally taken the pressure off of Gary, who might even tell you that he remembered your name. Regardless of whether he did or not, you played it right by taking him "off the hook" and allowing him to feel good about himself.

Step Number Ten: Introduce those you've met to each other. I call this "creative matchmaking" yet it has nothing to do with romance. It has more to do with setting up people to do business with each other, which will cause both to feel even better about you than they already do.

Let's pretend that while you are talking to Gary, Ann Jones, whom you met earlier, walks by. She sells telephone equipment to small businesses looking to expand their telecommunications abilities. Introduce her and Gary to each other first by name, and then by profession. Tell each what the other one does for work.

Now, do the ultimate in "people-building" by explaining to each how to know who would be a good prospect for the other. Wow! You can bet that no one has ever done that for them before. You have honored them by remembering their names, their professions, and even how to know how to find good prospects for them.

Now you're on a roll! You are positioning yourself as a true center of influence, and people will respond to what you project. All this time, you are just beginning to give them a hint that you're a person they definitely want to get to know.

Now you can even politely excuse yourself from the conversation and leave the two of them talking to each other. They will talk about the one common element in their lives up to this point . . . YOU! And, of course, how impressed they are with you. They still don't have a clue as to what you do. That's fine. They'll know as soon as you want them to know. When you are ready to approach them, they'll most likely be very interested in meeting with you.

Now we are ready for perhaps the most misunderstood yet most fun part of the process: the follow up. And we'll look at that in detail in the next chapter.

CHAPTER 3

Following Up

(Gently and Effectively)

Whether you met your prospect and began your "know you, like you, trust you" relationship through a chance meeting, a casual conversation (which we'll get to in the next chapter) or at a formal event such as the one described in the previous chapter, the stage is now set for you to progress to the follow–up portion of our prospecting system.

Many people are intimidated by follow-up. They imagine endless hours of unpleasantness such as data-base management, phone calls, and pestering behavior that is sure to turn off their prospects. Let's not do that.

We're going to pursue a follow-up strategy that is simple, easy, non-threatening – again, to both you and your prospect! – and very effective.

Incidentally, if you truly wanted to at this point, you certainly *could* call this person and invite them to look at the business. After the way you handled yourself with them, they may very well welcome you to show them your idea. And there will come a time when you will do this quite often because your names list will be so big, you'll just want to hurry and get people off your list as soon as possible.

So, you could call Gary the next day and reintroduce yourself. He'll remember you. Why wouldn't he? You made him feel great about himself. He might very well welcome you to show him your idea. You could then discuss with him what's happening with home-based businesses these days in terms of making money and income diversification, find out if he'd be interested in knowing how you are doing this for yourself, and – who knows – you might set an appointment.

But the chances of him agreeing to this are not nearly as good as they will be after you have gone through a couple of the follow-up methods we're about to discuss. So, unless your list is already huge, I suggest holding off on that call for just a bit longer.

ANOTHER GREAT *"FIRST"* IMPRESSION

Step Number One: Send a personalized, hand-written "thank you" note. Sure, we've all been taught to do that, but very few actually do it. People don't realize that in failing to follow through on this one step, they are missing out on a wonderful opportunity to niche themselves into the "feel-good" part of that person's mind. The set-up of this personalized notecard is as follows:

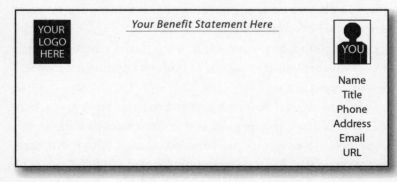

Actual size is 8 x 3-1/2 inches. Notice there is lots of space in which to write your note.

When he receives this note, he'll remember you positively for two main reasons: One is that you are probably the only one who has ever sent him this type of thank-you note (or possibly any thank-you note). The second reason is that your prospect will *see* who sent the note. Very important! More on that in a moment.

Regarding the description of your profession on your notecard, this is a touchy issue that can be handled in either of two ways. Since what is important is that your prospect feels good about *you* before you invite him to explore your business, you might want to highlight your J.O.B. on the notecard. Remember, it's only when you feel the time is appropriate for them to know about your Network Marketing business that he needs that information.

On the other hand, you *can* use your business name – either your independent contractor company name or the name of the actual company you represent (make sure and check first with the compliance department or your upline mentor) with a brief "benefit statement" across the bottom of the notecard.

If you do this, my suggestion would be to make the benefit statement about the *product* rather than about the *opportunity*.

You don't want to broadcast BUSINESS OPPORTUNITY, which can be a turnoff to some people. Choose which option works best for you. But – and this is a key point – before taking this to your printer, counsel with your upline mentorship regarding their advice on this issue.

The note you write to your new prospect should be brief, simple, non-pushy, and written in blue ink. Research indicates blue ink is more effective both in business and personally. The note should say something like, "Hi Gary, Thank you. It was a pleasure meeting you. If I can ever refer business your way, I certainly will." Then simply sign your name.

Insert your notecard into a standard #10 envelope and handwrite your prospect's name and address in blue ink, hand-stamp the envelope (no metered mail here; and large, commemorative stamps are best) and send. The fact that the envelope is handwritten and hand stamped practically ensures the envelope will be opened and your letter read, as opposed to falling the way of *junk mail*.

The Impression You've Made

Let's look at what you've done. First, you have again shown that you have a lot of class and are conscientious (building both your prospect's faith and trust in you). You've shown you are a person worthy of doing business with or referring to. In other words, you're a person worth getting to know.

What you didn't do was come on strong and try to hard sell, as do so many others. You simply thanked him for his time (we all like to be thanked, don't we?) and for the opportunity to have met. You also reaffirmed that you have his best interests in mind, letting him know you'll make an effort to send business his way.

Why Is The Picture So Important?
Because We Think in Pictures

Bob, I understand the reason for sending the note, but is it really important to include my picture?

Yes. As humans, we think in pictures; we remember in pictures. To prove this principle to yourself, simply try not to picture . . . a purple elephant. What comes to your mind?

Of course, a purple elephant, can't be avoided. And, if by chance you pictured a gray elephant, a blue elephant, or even a pink-polka-dotted elephant, it doesn't matter. You still pictured an elephant. Embrace this principle and use it to your advantage. Make sure your prospect has the opportunity to remember exactly who you are and is able to picture what you look like.

Know in advance that sending this notecard will not normally elicit a telephone call from this person, nor any type of instant gratification. But it raises the odds significantly that when you do decide to call him to set an appointment, he will be agreeable to meeting with you.

Again, at this point, if you choose, you *can* call him and invite him to look at the business in much the same way mentioned at the beginning of this chapter. And, soon you will want to do that. However, if you'll take the next couple of steps first, you'll increase your odds of setting an appointment even more dramatically.

Before we move on, I'd like to answer a question you may have, and that is, "Couldn't I have just sent my new prospect an email? After all, that's what everyone else does?"

Isn't it interesting how often the very answer you're looking for is contained within the question?

Yes, practically everyone is now using email. So, if you use it as well, does it separate you from everyone else? Hardly. Not to mention that it's also difficult (though not impossible) to include your picture in the email. Email is a fine communication tool, and you should make good use of it, but for the initial thank-you note, it absolutely pales in comparison to the handwritten notecard we just described.

KEEP THEM IN YOUR THOUGHTS

Step Number Two: Send any articles, newspaper or magazine clippings, or other pieces of information relating to your networking prospects personally or to their business. If you learn of something that might be helpful to them, send it on your personalized notecard.

For example, Gary (who sells copying machines) mentioned that he is an avid antique collector. You notice an article in your local newspaper about an antique shop going out of business that is making some extremely valuable collectibles available at bargain prices. Clip out the article, paperclip it to your personalized notecard, and write a brief note along the lines of, "Hi Gary, I remember you saying how much you enjoy antiques. Thought you might find this interesting." Then send it right out to him. Do you think he'll be impressed by your remembering him like that? You bet he will be!

Maybe you read about something that could help out Ann Jones. Remember her from the previous chapter? She sells telephone equipment to small businesses looking to expand their telecommunications abilities. Possibly you catch a tiny notice about a new office complex being built that will house small businesses. Perfect prospects for her! You might even do some reconnaissance work and find out who is handling the leasing.

Just send a note that says, "Hi Ann, came across the following item and thought it could be of value to you. Found out the building owner's name is Ms. Garrett. Her number is xxx-xxxx. Best of success, and great prospecting!" Then sign your name, put it in the envelope, stamp, and send. Simple, right? And do you think Ann might really appreciate your thought and effort? I bet she will. And, when you decide to call her because you'd like to run a business idea by her, do you think she'll be receptive? You can bet on that one, as well!

Step Number Three: Whenever you learn of a person having a particular want or need for a product or service, ask yourself, "Who do I know within my network of prospects that can fulfill those wants or needs?" This is probably the simplest and easiest of all the follow-up steps. It is nothing more than the mindset of continually helping others. It's also what will make you most memorable to them, and position you as a true center of influence within your community.

Soon you'll become that person everyone knows (not to mention likes and trusts). Before you know it, you are the person that others call because they've heard you know the answers; that you are the appropriate person who can help them. This might be for a particular product or service, but it also might be for something less direct. Possibly a mother or father wants to find their son or daughter a summer job at the town factory, and they don't know who to contact.

They've heard that if anyone would know, you would. And you know what; the fact is that even if you don't know, you know someone who would know. This is a result of the brilliant job you have done networking. You're well on your way to becoming a center of influence. And you are beginning to find that people are very receptive to meeting with you because of the positive reputation you have developed.

NOW IS THE TIME

Step Number Four: At this point, your list is growing so big and so fast that it's time to make those calls. Now, when you call, they know who you are. Inviting them is simply a matter of asking the right questions. You'll ask different prospects in different ways. Some you will want to meet with at their home and have an opportunity to share your business. A brief meeting at a coffee shop might be the best way to approach others. Still others you'll be able to invite straight to an open meeting. The choice is yours.

Phrasing the questions can also be different depending upon both the individual you are speaking with, and the methods for inviting prospects taught by your line of mentorship.

You may say, "Joanne, I'm in the process of expanding a business project with some very successful people. We're looking for an already successful entrepreneur – or whatever you sense this person perceives herself as being – who's open to other ways of (making money) or (diversifying their income) or (creating additional streams of income) or (interested in the idea of residual or royalty income)."

Use whichever of the preceding benefits that you believe best fits her situation. If she responds positively, great, set up the "visit." If she's not interested at this time, you can then ask her if she would be open to the idea of referring you to others who might be looking. If she enthusiastically responds that she would be open to that idea, then set a time you can get together to show her what you are doing. "Joanne, I know you're the type who before referring anyone, needs to know what it is you are referring them to." She'll most likely agree with that. Then, in order to show her what she'll be referring, you'll need to show her your business opportunity. Of course, while after seeing the business she might actually be interested herself, be sure that you respect her wishes. Explain the business to her *only* so that she is in a position to be able to enthusiastically refer you to others. If she then decides she's interested, that's simply a bonus. Later, we'll discuss how to ask for referrals properly so that the person is likely to be able to think of good, high-quality prospects who might benefit from your opportunity or products.

Repeat this pattern with those on the list with whom you decide to cultivate a relationship, and before long, you'll be exposing your awesome business to as many people as you'd like.

You might be asking, "This process obviously works, but is there any way to find and prospect people, and get to the point even quicker?"

Absolutely there is. And we'll discuss that in the next chapter.

CHAPTER 4

"QUICK" PROSPECTING
(Lots and Lots of Prospects)

Up to this point, I've tried to help you to add continually to your list of prospects and to overcome the feeling of being at a loss for finding new prospects. I've emphasized a method of prospecting that is not at all intimidating, either to you or to your prospects. As you've seen, it's a method that could effectively expand your inventory (your list of quality names) by 250 people every single time, and on a constant and continual basis.

Once you are at that point and are experiencing the effectiveness of this system, you will want to quicken the process a bit. In fact, you'll have such a huge list that your main goal will seem to be getting people off your list just as fast as you're putting them on. That mindset makes prospecting very, very fun. And very, very comfortable.

Why? Well, remember earlier we talked about and defined posture? True posture is when you care, but not that much. In other words, you have so many names on your list and people to talk to, that if someone isn't interested, you are pretty much "outta there" (respectfully, of course, both to them and in your own mind). Before they complete the word "no," you're mentally on to the next person. What a great feeling!

With that in mind, let's go to some great places for meeting lots of quality people. Our goal in this chapter is to quickly establish relationships, ask a couple qualifying questions, and then deciding whether to bring the business up right now, or simply get their business card and call them to set up a visit. (Remember, you can always opt to go through the follow-up process described in the last chapter if you feel more comfortable doing that.)

CAPPUCCINO ANYONE?

As we mentioned in Chapter two, an excellent place to prospect is one of the super-bookstores (the ones that have a separate section for people to read while drinking coffee), or even an upscale coffee shop. Both of these venues tend to have a large number of upscale, ambitious, quality people frequenting their establishments. These are the people to keep your eye on.

Let's explore prospecting at the bookstore in more detail.

Step Number One: Relax at one of the tables with a cup of coffee, a latte, a cappuccino, or whatever else suits your fancy, and take out a book to read. Enjoy yourself, and the experience, knowing that there is absolutely no pressure for you to meet anyone special. When it's ready to happen, it will happen.

Step Number Two: Notice a sharp-looking person sitting down at a table near you who begins to read a book, enjoying their coffee, latte, cappuccino, or whatever suits *their* fancy.

Step Number Three: Make eye contact, smile and say "hello." Say something *original* such as, "Good cappuccino isn't it?" (Not exactly brain surgery here, is it?)

Step Number Three (addition): Any other conversation starter will do. For instance, "What are you reading?" If the person responds in a cheerful, welcoming way, you can begin to discuss their book, asking questions about it if you haven't yet read it or bringing up a certain point about it if you have. You can make a comment question such as, "aren't books great?" and then begin a very positive discussion about books.

Step Number Four: Eventually, your conversation will progress to the point where you ask what line of work they're in, and then you can ask a couple of the *Feel-good Questions*™ we discussed earlier. Remember the first two; "How did you get started in the widget business?" and "What do you enjoy most about what you do?"

THE ONE "KEY" STATEMENT

Step Number Four: Say the "One Key Statement." Whereas in the previous scenario (see Chapter two) you asked the "One Key Question," "How can I know if someone I'm talking to would be a good prospect for you?" (Of course, you could still ask that question now if you so choose.) Here you are going to do something different. You're going to gently reach out to your prospect with a statement that will both qualify their interest in looking at a new business idea, and provide you with an appropriate response to their response.

This one key statement is:

"You must really love what you do!" (Or something similar.)

Here is what you have just accomplished: First, you continued to make your prospect feel encouraged and good about the conversation. Secondly, there is no way they will feel defensive, because prospecting questions (that is, the kind to which people react defensively) usually sound as though they are attempting to elicit dissatisfaction. Your question showed admiration and respect.

Your prospect will more than likely respond to your statement in either one of two ways, and either way is fine.

Response #1: "Yes, I do love my work. It's been great. Very enjoyable and rewarding."

To this you can respond. "You know what's fascinating? If there's one thing I've learned it's that people such as yourself who are already successful, are always the ones who are open to {other ways of making more money} or {new business ideas and strategies}."

To your response, your prospect will either respond by saying:

"No, not I." Or, "Yes, definitely. Why, what are you working on?"

Both answers are fine. One doesn't waste your time (or theirs), and the other presents you with an opportunity to introduce your business opportunity, if that's what you choose to do at this time.

You might say, "I'm in the process of expanding a business project with some very successful people in the area. It's already showing tremendous growth potential, and we're looking for a few more leaders to work with us. Would you want to know more?" Use any words or phrases that you feel are relevant to your prospect, based on his or her personal situation.

Again, you'll get either a yes or a no, and you can proceed from there. This takes care of response number one. Now . . .

Response #2: "No, I hate what I do. I'm not making near the income I should be making. It's very frustrating. I'd rather be doing something else."

To this you can respond, "You know, it's interesting. Some people such as yourself are obviously very sharp and have a lot of income potential, but they're simply affiliated with the wrong vehicle." When they agree (which they probably will), now go into the part regarding the business you are expanding.

Depending upon your feelings about the situation, environment, timing, whatever, you can introduce the business right there, or get their card and let them know you'll call them when you're able to in order to set a business meeting. Your posture is excellent.

Do this with enough new people, and your inventory will expand exponentially; so too, eventually, will your organization.

CHAPTER 5

TYING IT ALL TOGETHER (SO FAR)

(Remember the Fundamentals)

You've got it. Just keep it simple, and don't put any undue pressure on yourself. Practice this process a few times, and before long, you're utilizing a method that can't possibly fail to put as many people in front of the business as it'll take for you to succeed.

BUILD ON YOUR SMALL SUCCESSES

Remember to build on your small successes. If going through the entire process as described in Chapter two seems somewhat daunting right now, then take it one step at a time. For instance, instead of having to meet five people and engage them in full conversations complete with *Feel-Good Questions*™, just say "hello" to five different people. Or to just one person. Do that and you've won.

Now begin to build on that small success. Next event you go to, say hello to seven people and introduce yourself to five people. Awesome – you're doing great!

Next event, say "hello" to ten people, introduce yourself to seven, and engage one person in the entire process. See what's happening??!!

Now you are ready to meet people in any type of situation and just begin lighthearted conversations in which you ask some open-ended, *Feel-Good Questions*™, you let them talk about themselves, and get some business cards. Then the simple, easy and effective follow-up process begins.

UTILIZE THE SYSTEM

The good news for you is that the correct way – a proven, duplicable system – for building your business is already there for you. It consists of mentor-recommended books, CDs, seminars, major conventions, voicemail, and three-way calls. Where else can you, for such a relatively small amount of money, have access to millionaires and multi-millionaires who have successfully accomplished what you are looking to accomplish. My suggestion is not to challenge the system and try to shortcut it, but to embrace it, and let it help you accomplish your goals and dreams.

If you'll follow the method outlined in this booklet, plug into the system endorsed by your company leadership, and work hand-in-hand with your upline mentors, yes, you'll still have problems in your life . . . but money and time will not be two of them!

In the following chapters, we'll continue to look at other methods of cultivating new, A-list prospects. But, if you just did what we've discussed so far, you'll be well on your way.

But, why stop there?

CHAPTER 6

REFERRALS

The concept of referrals is just a bit different in Network Marketing than it is from traditional sales. Of course, the good news is that basic success principles always stay the same. So, after a brief look at the difference, let's go right to utilizing one of the best forms of leverage there is . . . OPSI (Other Peoples' Sphere of Influence).

When you bring a new associate into your business, his prospects (at least the ones you had initially contacted) are, in a sense, referrals. So, in this chapter, we won't worry about that because they are also your prospects!

When we discuss referrals in this chapter, we'll look at it in two ways:

1. The referrals of potential business builders from someone to whom you've shown the business

opportunity but who, at this time, is not personally interested in joining the business.

2. Customers who are currently enjoying your com-
    pany's products and/or services.

Regarding situation #1, many people don't see this as being
a viable source of referrals. Well, tell that to John, whose last
two qualifying legs for the top level with his company were
the direct results of referrals from people who said "no" to the
opportunity!

The key is that they saw the opportunity as being terrific
but, for reasons of their own, chose not to join. Still, they
had enough respect for John (they knew him, liked him, and
trusted him) that they felt very good about referring him to
others who might in fact be interested.

When it comes to situation #2, however, there practically
isn't anyone who can't see the advantages of doing this. After
all, with the technology of automatic ordering and shipping
as it is today at the state of the art, why wouldn't any Network
Marketer want to increase the number of customers in their
business. It's an excellent profit center.

Plus, you never know when one of these ecstatically happy
product/service users will decide it's time for them to build the
business. And, even if they personally don't, the more customers to whom they refer you, the greater the chances some of
them will eventually decide to pick up on the business opportunity aspect.

Since the actual asking for referrals is by and large the same
whether it's for both of the above situations, let's focus for now
on the second one; a customer from whom you'd like to receive,
via referrals, lots of other potential customers.

This will happen as a result, not only of asking for referrals, but of asking for referrals . . . correctly!

Years ago, shortly after I had joined a company's local sales force, the sales manager held a meeting one morning focusing on how to increase referrals. The question he asked was, "How do you get referrals?" One of the young salespeople who had just come over from another company was supposed to be a real dynamo. He immediately threw up his hand and said, all-knowingly, "You ask for them!"

To my amazement, the sales manager said, "That's right." I remember thinking to myself, "How naive!" Actually, they were both half right. You do have to ask. Where they missed the boat is this: You have to do more than just ask. You must ask in a way that provides a meaningful opportunity for that person to be able to come up with quality names.

THE MOST COMMON MISTAKE

You see, the biggest mistake most people make in asking for referrals is that they think – not too big but – too wide. Here's what I mean.

Have you ever asked someone, either after a sale, or at any other time when you really felt good about this person wanting to help you: "Kay, do you know anybody else who could benefit from my products or services?"

I'll bet Kay began to stare off into space. I mean, she was thinking about it—and thinking about it in earnest, really concentrating. After all, she wanted to help you, as well as help those she cared about whom you'd be serving via your terrific products or services. Finally, she said, "Well, I can't think of anybody right now, but when I do, I'll definitely let you know."

You then probably never heard from her again regarding a referral.

It wasn't Kay's fault. She just wasn't asked in a way that would help her find the answer.

When we ask people "who do you know who..." or do you "know anyone who..." we are giving them much too large – or wide – a frame of reference. A blurry collage of 250 faces (their sphere of influence) will run through their mind, but no individuals will stand out. They might feel frustrated, like they're letting you down. And, the more pressure they put on themselves to think of someone, the less the chances are they'll be able to do so..

Here's the solution: find a way to funnel their world down to just a few people. We've got to give them a frame of reference that they can work with.

Have You Heard the One about the...

Let me explain it this way. Has anybody ever asked you if you knew any good jokes? Now, you probably know plenty of good jokes, but can you actually think of one when someone asks you? I can't.

Here's another example. One night I called my local golden oldies radio station and requested a particular song. The announcer told me they no longer carry that song on their play list. "But" he asked, "Do you happen to know any other oldies you'd like to hear?" I can tell you right now that I know hundreds of oldies I'd like to hear, but could I think of even one at that moment? No way!

It's the same when we ask people if they know "anybody" who could benefit from our products or services. Most likely they know plenty of people who could, or who might. Try to get them to think of even one person at that time using that methodology, however, and it's probably not going to happen.

THE SOLUTION IS TO ISOLATE

In his classic, *How to Master the Art of Selling*, Tom Hopkins suggests that instead, you provide the person with a frame of reference; actually, several frames of reference, but all small enough that the person can actually *see* individuals in their "mind's eye."

Let's take the following example. You are talking to Joe, a Center of Influence in your community. Joe really likes you. You've sent him business, provided him with some background information for one of his projects, and, who knows, maybe you even fixed him up with a blind date that worked out. You are well aware, through asking the right questions during previous conversations that Joe happens to be a golfing enthusiast. Let's look at how we might approach this situation with Joe.

YOU: Joe, you were telling me you're an avid golfer.

JOE: Yes, I am. Been playing for over 20 years. If I ever get to retire, I'll probably play every day. Right now, though, it's only on weekends. And I mean, every weekend.

YOU: Hmm. Is there a specific foursome you play with most of the time?

JOE: Well, yeah, there's Joe Martin, Harry Browne and Nancy Goldblatt.

YOU: Joe, as far as you know, would any of them be people I should speak to?

Now, it might be that none of the three Joe mentioned are either good prospects at this particular time or at least people to whom he'd feel comfortable referring you to contact, but at least you are increasing his odds of being able to help you. You gave him three people he could *see*.

Now let's move along to the next frame of reference.

YOU: How long have you been involved with your local Rotary Club?

JOE: About six years now. Great bunch of people.

YOU: Joe, are there one or two people in your club that you tend to sit next to every meeting? [Notice you didn't ask, "Does anyone in your club need..." It might be a large club, thus you would be right back with the same problem of too many people for him to be able to isolate anyone.]

JOE: Really just one person—Mike O'Brien. Been friends with him and his family for years.

YOU: Do you think Mike would be someone who could benefit from my...?

Again, maybe yes, maybe no. Regardless, let's look at just one more frame.

Perhaps Joe is on the board of directors of his local professional association. Again, instead of asking if anyone in the association would fit the type of profile you're looking for, ask him how many people serve on the board of directors with him. Suppose the answer is five. Five is a small enough number for him to handle and be able to visualize each person.

YOU: Joe, picture those five. Do you feel any of them would be open to knowing about...?

Do you see where we're going with this? Somewhere within the frames of reference you're providing, one or several people will come to mind. In effect, while you're limiting the number of people in his world from whom to choose, you are actually increasing the number of people he'll be able to identify and provide as referrals. Very effective.

And understand, once you get the first couple of names, you'll start working your way out to include as many people as possible. What's interesting is that once he gives you that first person's name—and that first one is the most difficult—from there, it's a piece of cake.

Between your helping him to identify people, and then one name breaking the ice and each successive name triggering his memory of someone else he knows, all of a sudden, that trickle of names becomes a stream, which becomes a gushing fountain, and then you're literally sitting back and taking names.

See how fun this can get?

Important point: While the person is giving you these names, don't worry about any additional information, such as telephone numbers, email addresses, points of qualification, or anything else. There's plenty of time for that once Joe has exhausted his list of names. While he's giving them to you, just write the names down. After he's through, *then* you have the option of asking for whatever additional information you feel might be helpful.

Remember, too, you can inquire about which neighbors he has relationships with and could introduce you to. You can also help him to identify others by simply running the "occupation alphabet" we discussed in Chapter One, asking them who they know who is an accountant, a banker, a chiropractor, a dentist, an engineer, and so forth. The more you have this already worked out in your head before your actual conversation, the more confident and effective you will be.

I remember my delight in seeing that, after the original edition of my book, (*Endless Referrals: Network Your Everyday Contacts into Sales*) was published, a young man who had just become involved in Network Marketing posted a review on Amazon.com stating that utilizing this particular method of asking for referrals, he received 23 referrals from a center of influence just a week after he met him.

Once you begin getting comfortable with this process, you'll be astounded by the number of high-quality referrals you get. Your retail business becomes a good deal of fun – not to mention, profitable, at that point. It won't always happen as quickly as it did for this young man, but it doesn't have to happen that quickly all the time for it to still be hugely successful.

You might be wondering if this will seem pushy. The answer is no, not if this person has genuine good feelings about you and wants to see you succeed.

When seeking referrals, you want to make it as easy as possible for a referrer-source to refer you. Know the frame-of-reference questions you are going to ask before you ask them. If you feel comfortable with the process, they will too.

CHAPTER 7

SETTING REFERRAL-BASED APPOINTMENTS

It's one thing to obtain the referral - it's quite another to successfully set the appointment with the person to whom you were referred. Despite the fact that someone your referred prospect knows, likes, and trusts referred you, it's still easy to imagine what might be going on in his or her head.

- "I don't want to be bothered by a salesperson."

- "I don't need whatever he/she is selling."

- "Is this person going to try to 'hard-sell' me on buying their product or service?"

- "Am I about to hear a 'pitch' for a Network Marketing opportunity?" (Heaven-forbid)

With that in mind, let's look at how we can invite people in a way that is non-intimidating and non-threatening, and very effective.

By the way, although, in the last chapter we discussed referrals primarily from the viewpoint of product and customers, let's go back to focusing on business-builders. The reason is that, for potential product buyers, setting an appointment to discuss products is not as difficult. Either the referral source will have raved about them or you can mention a quick benefit or two and they'll either be interested in learning more or not. And, you'll begin to have so many new prospects, you won't care. (Of course, you will care . . . but not that much!).

For this, let's pretend you've shared the business with someone named Steve who, at this time, is not interested. However, you were able to elicit several referrals from Steve. Here's how your call to your referred prospect might sound.

YOU: Ms. Prospect, this is Sue Johnson. I believe you know Steve Abbott.

RP (REFERRED PROSPECT): Yes, how is he?

YOU: Great. Actually, I was speaking with him the other night and your name came up in conversation.

RP: Really? How?

YOU: I'm in the process of expanding a business project with some very successful people, and we're looking for some already-successful people such as you to expand with us. I can't necessarily promise that it'll be a fit, but Steve spoke highly of you and suggested I call. Would you like to meet for a quick cup of coffee and I'll run it past you?

RP: Sounds interesting. Can you tell me a little bit about it first?

You: Absolutely. We're expanding an internet, e-commerce-based project (or whatever it is you do) and it'll be simple to draw it out for you in person. Again, we'll know better whether or not it's a fit once we meet.

Let's look at just a few of the elements that were involved. First, you immediately put your prospect at ease by immediately referencing your referral source. Then, using what I call "quick language" (it isn't said quickly but implies it won't take a lot of time) you let her know the meeting wouldn't take too long ("quick cup of coffee"). When she asked you for more information, you didn't try and hide what you were doing (although the "curiosity approach" has its place, it's not advisable to go 100 percent with it as many Network Marketers still do). Naturally, you can't present the business, or the products, over the telephone any more than a doctor could do a checkup and provide a diagnosis over the telephone. But you still need to give the person an idea of what it's about. This works out for both of you, as you'll be able to pre-qualify potential interest without giving away so much information that your prospect will make a major decision with very little relevant information. Those types of decisions usually result in a "no."

One of my original prospecting mentors, Rick Hill suggests giving the prospect a "back door" so that he will feel totally comfortable with you, and not at all pressured. At a certain point in the conversation, often right near the beginning, he'll say:

"By the way, Peggy didn't assume you'd be interested and, personally, neither do I. She just thought that you might like to take a look at a business idea we discussed. We could meet for a quick cup of coffee and I'll run the idea past you."

The key part of that statement is, "Peggy didn't assume you'd be interested and, personally, neither do I."

Can you imagine a less threatening way to approach someone on the telephone? You've just told them they might not be interested, so there's nothing for them to feel defensive about.

And, again, the "quick cup of coffee" and "I'll 'run' the idea past you" are very effective (providing they're true). In today's fast-paced world, where people perceive themselves as being too busy, that kind of language assures them you won't take up any more of their valuable time than necessary.

Putting your referred prospect at ease, by both a lack of pressure and a minimal infringement on their time, will help you greatly to increase the odds of setting the appointment.

Set the appointment, and then you can help that person derive the benefits from your exceptional opportunity. And, if not that, perhaps your product or service. And, while you're at it, you can get some more referrals, as well.

CHAPTER 8

THREE-WAY CALLS
(Easy as ABC)

Three-way calls (also known as ABC calls, where your upline mentor is "A", you are "B", and your prospect is "C") are one of the most effective methods of moving a prospect to the next step in the information process. Yet, very few people utilize this powerful tool. Why? Two reasons stand out. One is that people feel they are "bothering" their upline mentor. The other is that most people find it difficult to gain agreement from the prospect to participate in this type of communication. We'll address both. First, however, why are three-way calls so effective?

The power of a three-way call is based on the principle that, as human beings, we tend to perceive less credibility in those we know than in people who are total strangers. It's simply human nature. Thus; your prospect will perceive you to be less credible than someone they've not yet met. Again, that's just how it is. We can either fight that principle (and lose out on a wonderful business-building mechanism), or embrace it. Let's choose the latter.

RATIONAL SELF-INTEREST: THE PROFIT MOTIVE

So you don't want to bother your upline mentor with three-way calls. Let's analyze this. If you felt that your three-way call would also help your upline mentor, would you feel differently? Sure you would. Well, guess what . . . it does! Here's why: Your upline has a profit motive in helping you build your business. By helping you build a huge, residual-based business, he or she is helping their business as well. That's the beauty of Network Marketing. One only helps themselves by helping those in their organization.

By the way; knowing that you have a rational self-interest in your organization calling you for 3-ways, does it now make total sense that the best thing you could do for your upline mentor is to "bother" them as much as possible? Good! Bother them. They want you to.

NOW, THE HOW TO

Here is where many get stuck. Various questions in this area range from "How to get someone to agree to a three-way (in other words, the prospect saying, 'No, I don't really need to speak to anyone else – I already understand enough')," to "How do you make a natural transition from a conversation to suggesting a three-way call?".

What's best is to actually set up the three-way from the very beginning of your initial presentation. How? After quickly determining who the proper upline person will be with whom to do the three-way (you'll judge who will be most relatable to your individual prospect), begin to edify them. To "Edify" means to build. Verbally build your upline mentor to your prospect from the beginning of your conversation. Do so to the point where the one person in the world your prospect would like to meet is your upline mentor (key point: this must be done with honesty and sincerity, which is why it is so vitally important to develop and cultivate upline relationships).

During your follow-up call to review the reasons (based on your initial conversation) why your prospect is interested, again edify your upline. Then simply let them know you're going to introduce them to someone they'd like to meet. "Hold on just a moment. I'm going to see if I can get Jane on the phone real-quick to say hello to you. Hold on just a second."

Let's review. First, you transitioned into the three-way invite in a very natural way. This takes the pressure off your prospect that you have "methodically planned out a double-team attack." Then you phrased the invite in a way that you are doing it for him, not for you. Next, you – key point – didn't ask his permission ("hold on just a moment. I'm gonna . . ."), leaving it up to his judgment as to whether he wants to participate. Remember, he doesn't yet know why this call is so important.

You then used what I referred to in the previous chapter as "quick language" (" . . . on the phone real-quick to say hello to you. Hold on just a second.")

Finally, although you didn't ask permission, you also certainly didn't force or coerce him into the three-way call, which would simply not be right. You left enough time for him to refuse before you put him on hold (that is important), but at the same time, you set it up so that your prospect must make a conscious and active decision to say "no" as opposed to making a decision to say "yes."

DOUBLE EDIFICATION

Now edify them both, and then let your upline mentor take over and "do the work for you." First you'll edify your upline, the "A", fitting right into what you've told your prospect. Then – and this is powerful – edify your prospect. Example (let's pretend Jane is your upline mentor and Steve is your prospect): "Jane, this is Steve. He's a very successful business owner and community leader. We've discussed (name of company) a couple of times. I'm very impressed with him, and could see him really 'tearing up' this business. Jane, Steve; I'm gonna sort of step back and let you two say hello.

Now let your upline mentor take over. Completely! Don't interrupt or try to "save her" by jumping in and filling in any key words "she might have forgotten" (that's de-edifying). Just relax and know that she'll do what she does best – edify you and the business to your prospect. Pretty soon you will be the "A", your current prospect will be the "B", and you'll get to do the same thing for them and their "C."

Let the power of the three-way call work for you . . . and your prospect!

CHAPTER 9

OBJECTIONS

(They May Be More Than Just What They Seem) (Okay, And Answering Them, Too)

While the gist of this book is "finding, meeting and winning over" the new people you meet in order to develop a huge list of quality prospects, let's face it; it's also important to be prepared for the objections you'll receive once you're doing the presentation (or even during the inviting).

So, if you don't mind, I'll address that in this chapter by way of an article I wrote for an industry magazine for which I sometimes write. It goes as follows:

A brand new Network Marketer emailed me with the following question:

"Dear Bob,
I'm involved with a Network Marketing company that I really believe is a good value. Recently I was sharing it with someone and they said 'I cannot afford to join.'

"Bob, I know that the small outlay of $320 can and will be the best investment they make. So how can I make them realize this and handle that objection best? In other words, what would be the best method and comeback to this objection?

"I feel that they can NOT afford not to join and I feel that they may even have the money but are making excuses to not join. I guess my question is, 'What is a good statement to make to that objection?'"

Dear Reader,

First, congratulations on finding and joining a Network Marketing company you believe in. That is certainly the first step toward your success and in touching the lives of many others. Make sure you learn the "system" utilized by the top associates in your company so you can duplicate their success. I also appreciate the fact that you're doing your research and wanting to know the best way to handle objections your prospects will give you.

Actually, the question you asked is based on one of the typical objections you'll regularly receive as a Network Marketer.

Basically, they include:

1. I can't afford it

2. I don't have the time

3. I can't sell

4. I've been in one of these before and it didn't work

5. This is a Pyramid Scheme

And there are several others.

All of these objections have logical, as you called them, "comebacks" you can use (as an important point, however, what we need to work on are "responses" as opposed to "comebacks" – responses position you both on the "same side" while comebacks are more combative in nature).

The challenge posed by *comebacks* is threefold:

1. They are usually logical, and people don't buy (in this case, "buy" means to take action and join) based on logic, but upon emotion.

2. They (comebacks) can appear to be argumentative, which is why it's important to answer any questions/objections with tact and diplomacy. I refer to this as "Winning Without Intimidation."

3. Comebacks often answer the asked objection, but not the real one. For instance, as you alluded to in your email, when you said they may have the money but are making excuses not to join. So, your perfect comeback may be answering an objection they don't actually have, while unintentionally ignoring the real one.

So, while my first suggestion is (as usual) to get with your upline mentor and ask them how to answer these objections as best relates to your particular company, products, services and situation, I'd also like to share with you a couple of brief thoughts:

#1 Keep in mind what someone is *truly* communicating when they tell you they don't have $320 to join. They are really saying, "Based on what I (don't) know about the potential of this industry and business opportunity and what I (don't) understand about the company, I don't believe it's worth $320 of my hard-earned money.

So, it might mean that, within the presentation, you haven't built up the benefits of your business enough for them to understand the potential. If they thought the potential was $100,000, would they not be able to afford $320? Are you building the dream enough during your presentation? Are you offering them compelling evidence, backed by third-party testimonials?

Another thought is this; there are a lot of people out there; do you really want to work with the people who will not part with $320 to involve themselves in a lucrative business? If you do, why do you? One thing about Ultra-successful Network Marketers is that they treat it as a business first. In business, you qualify people. As Michael Dorsey and Mike Lemire say, "Pros don't convince; they sort."

Personally, I'd rather see you pursue people who are already ambitious and willing to do what it takes to succeed, as opposed to people you have to drag into it. They are the ones who are most likely going to need constant babysitting and attention, and could hold you back. You should be looking for potential leaders.

That said, let's look at a generic way to handle an objection, using the one you brought up as our example:

First, with kindness, turn their objection into a question. You can do this by saying, "Tom, that's an excellent question. And it's a very worthy one." Here you've explained that it's more of a question that can be answered as opposed to a stopping point. And, you complimented him on his "thought-provoking" question. Now he is much more likely to drop his defensive stance, realizing he will not be "attacked" for his question.

Next, use a variation of the "Feel, Felt and Found" technique ("I understand how you feel, many others have felt the same way, until they found that..."). I say a "variation" of such because so many people know of this method that it can sound contrived, and nothing will break rapport with a prospect quicker and more completely than when they feel they are being "techniqued."

Instead, say something similar to "I can relate to your question, and I'm sure many others can, as well. After all, this is a different type of business model than one with which you're familiar. What so many now-financially-free people have discovered, however, Tom, is that for the relatively tiny financial investment in this business compared to traditional businesses, the payoff is extraordinarily high."

From here, you can, if necessary, explain further why this is so.

One more thing: Try and avoid the trap many Network Marketers fall into, and that is "wanting it – success – for your prospects more than they want it for themselves." In other words, some people are happy where they are; some people are miserable where they are, and others are happy being miserable where they are. Your job is to offer them a vehicle, and opportunity, not to insist that they take it. That is up to them. Of course, if they do take it, and truly desire to succeed, then you can match their desire.

A dear friend and mentor of mine and perhaps the greatest speaker of all time, Bill Gove, once told me that we are responsible "to" others, but not "for" them. In other words, your responsibility is to offer your excellent opportunity to everyone you feel would benefit. Give them the facts, build their dream and do the best you can to help them become involved. At the same time, realize that their life choices are "their" life choices, not yours, and honor them and their decision, whatever it happens to be. Then go sponsor someone who is looking!

Congratulations again on joining an industry that can help set you free, as you understand "free" to be, while you help others to accomplish that same goal for themselves.

CHAPTER 10

ANSWER OBJECTIONS AND PERSUADE YOUR PROSPECT

(By Not Answering Objections And By Not Persuading Your Prospects)

Here's something to keep away from: Answering objections. At least the way most people do. Here are some examples: *"I don't have the time to do this business. I don't have enough hours in the day to do the things I need to do right now."*

"Sure you do. After all, everybody has at least a couple of hours a night if they really want to have the things they can have through this business. Besides, if you don't have the time now, what makes you think you'll have any more time to enjoy your life five years from now?!"

"I can't sell."

"Of course you can sell. You sell every day. Aren't you selling when you try to persuade your spouse to go to the restaurant you want to go to? Or when you try to get your child to study harder in school? Or when you hit your boss up for a raise? Of course you can sell. You always sell!"

"Isn't this like a pyramid?"

"No, a pyramid is illegal. Besides, isn't your current job like a pyramid? Only in that pyramid only the people at the top make all the money and you can never surpass that person's income. In this business you're at the top of your own organization and you can actually make more money than the people who got in before you?"

How many times have you faced those objections, responded to them and convinced the person that you were right and they were wrong . . . and then he or she still never joined the business?

One reason this happened is because you were attempting to persuade a person who didn't want to be persuaded. Actually, not many people enjoy being persuaded because that would entail their changing their mind.

As Zig Ziglar says (slightly paraphrased), "Contrary to popular belief, people don't change their mind. Instead, they make new decisions, based on new information."

And he's so right.

Often, you'll notice that the leaders in this business are those who have a knack for letting people come to their own conclusions and their own decisions. They know it's true that, as Dale Carnegie said, "A person convinced against their will is of the same opinion still."

I believe the following is a basic principle of human action:

"A person is much more likely to agree with a statement they make than a statement you (or I) make."

Allow me to share something that happened a while back. While the situation has nothing to do with the business, I believe the principle involved does.

Tammi, a 19 year old waitress at a local restaurant I often frequent, was complaining of a headache. I shared with her a remedy I once learned that sounds rather odd but has worked amazingly well for everyone with whom I've shared it – cutting a cold lime in half and rubbing the juicy part all over your forehead. I don't know why it works, but it does (then again, I don't know why, when I flip on the light switch, the lights go on, but I do it anyway because it works).

Well, Tammi is the type who generally doesn't believe anything. So when I made the suggestion, she laughed and waved the idea away with her hand.

Now, Tammi's a real good kid and I hated to see her suffer needlessly with a headache. My initial "reaction" was to say, in aggravated voice, "Tammi, what have you got to lose – just try it!"

Tell me though, had I done that, do you think it would have worked? Would she have said, "Oh, Bob, what a great idea. Just try it. Why didn't I think of that?"

We both know the odds are about 99.9 percent she would not have. Instead, she would have remained resistant to the idea. So, I didn't say anything . . . and waited for another opportunity.

About five minutes later, as she was refilling my water glass she said, "It's funny, I once heard of this great cure for the hiccups which really works. All you do is...." and she told me what it was.

(Come to think of it, I don't remember what the cure was. I do remember that it sounded even stranger than rubbing the juicy part of a lime over your forehead to relieve a headache.)

Here was my opportunity. And there were various "potential" responses, both helpful and non-helpful, I could offer. Let's analyze a few of them.

1. "Well, Tammi, why would you believe something foolish like that instead of what I told you about the lime?"

While this is the natural response, it certainly won't cause the desired action. It's attacking the person's ego and saying, "I should be listened to but you shouldn't be."

2. "I'll tell you what; you try the lime right now and next time I have the hiccups, I'll try your idea."

Though a little better than #1, it's still patronizing and is ego-based. Not likely to be effective. More likely to elicit a polite laugh from the other person – but not the desired action.

3. After listening to her suggestion very attentively, I said, "Wow, what a neat idea. I'll definitely try that next time I get the hiccups. Thank you."

Of course, that is what I actually said to her and her response was, "You know what, let me go find a lime and see if it works" (which she did....and it did).

Why did #3 work when we all know that the first two probably would not have?

As usual, it was mainly a matter of showing another person the proper respect and treating her as a responsible, self-directing individual with the ability to make the best decision for herself.

And, there was one more thing. Instead of trying to pro-actively persuade her to my way of thinking, I held back (not always easy to do) and allowed her to come to her own conclusion. Her suggestion to me merely allowed me to demonstrate to her that that is what I was doing.

Sometimes it's simply necessary to use positive detachment and allow ourselves to not have to have the answer; to not have to "actively persuade." In time - hopefully sooner but sometimes later - that person, seeing and sensing the respect we've given them, will be more open to our suggestion.

This does not mean that you ignore an objection, don't respond to it, and then leave it to the person to all of a sudden come up with the answer. What it does mean is that perhaps you open the question up to discussion first by agreeing with them, understanding their point, and then asking questions which will elicit their answering their own objection.

Let's take one of the objections we heard earlier:

"Isn't this like a pyramid?"

"I don't know. I guess it depends on how we'd define a pyramid. What does a pyramid seem like it would be to you?"

"Well, the person at the top makes the money and the rest do all the work."

"That's a great point. Does that remind you of anyplace you're familiar with?"

"It sort of reminds me of exactly where I work."

Your prospect has just answered the first part of his own objection. He now knows that a pyramid is where he works. Now let's take it a step further.

"Now let's draw out what our organization might look like (draw out where the person higher on the chart than he is has a certain size group, but his has a lot more people)." Then ask:

"Who do you think should be making more income in this diagram?"

"The person whose built a bigger group."

"Yes. And that's exactly what happens here."

"Oh, that's different than what I thought."

Yes, sometimes the most effective way to persuade someone is not to "actively persuade" at all. Instead, let them persuade themselves.

And, sometimes, the most effective way to answer an objection is to not answer it at all. Instead, let them answer it themselves. Of course, you can help.

As the saying goes, "Even though you can lead a horse to water but cannot make him drink . . . you can still salt his oats and make him thirsty."

CHAPTER 11

SYSTEMS
LEAD TO SUCCESS

In my booklet, *The Success Formula* (which you can read for free at www.TheSuccessFormula.com), I make the point that a key to success in any area in which one might desire to succeed (i.e., building a business, losing weight, improving relationships, lowering a golf score, etc.), is using a "System" that's been proven to work . . . and simply duplicating that system.

As master author and speaker, Brian Tracy advises, "Just find out what successful people do, and do the same things, until you get the same results." Yes, it really is that simple (though "simple" should never be confused with easy).

I personally define a "System" as "The process of 'predictably' achieving a goal based on a logical and specific set of how-to principles." According to Michael Gerber, author of The E-Myth (paraphrased), "Systems permit ordinary people to achieve extraordinary success, predictably."

There's a saying Network Marketing leaders accurately use to advise those within their organization who try to "shortcut" the system by not using the right tools or only following the steps with which they feel comfortable:

"Don't try and shortcut the system, because the system is the shortcut."

In their book, *The Millionaire Real Estate Agent*, the authors, Gary Keller, Dave Jenks and Jay Papasan, when discussing the concept of "System" say, "Systems are simply the repeatable processes that allow us to duplicate magnificent results easily."

WOW - I love it! (Yes, of course the real estate business is different from the Network Marketing business but "Success Principles" are "Success Principles" regardless of what is being discussed. Would you agree?)

There's one aspect of teaching the importance of using systems, however, that is always a challenge. That is trying to get people, when learning a system, to stay with the basics, the fundamentals, and not to get too creative. Especially at first.

But, Bob, are we supposed to be robots, never doing anything different?

The answer: Not at all. Though, before one is ready to get creative, one first needs to absolutely know the basics, the fundamentals. It's extremely important to base creativity on a foundation of knowledge and wisdom.

What a system will do, in any area of your life, is allow you to accomplish your goals in a much more predictable fashion.

While creativity is a very worthwhile aspect of life, it seems as though creativity - in order to be effective - is best built upon the basic fundamentals. Every magnificent move Michael Jordan ever made on a basketball court was a derivative of the most fundamental aspect of the sport - dribbling the basketball.

One of my favorite business quotes is from a mega-successful entrepreneur (and I wish I remembered his name so I could properly credit him). He said: "I've never been much interested in being on the leading edge of creativity. However, I've always been fascinated by being on the leading edge of . . . profitability." This holds true whether "profit" is meant in terms of money or any other worthwhile accomplishment.

For example, if your goal is to lose 20 pounds (as mine was a couple years ago) do you care if you do so following a proven system or making up your own? Personally, I just wanted to lose the weight in the quickest, most efficient manner that would allow me to then keep it off and be healthy. Since I personally lacked the knowledge to do so on my own, I chose to follow someone else's system and it worked. What I did not do was to start out with that system and then change it as I went along. How counter-productive that would have been.

Weight loss author and consultant, Julia Griggs Havey, who herself lost 185 pounds and now successfully teaches her system to people world-wide and Donna Krech, author and owner of a chain of the renowned "Thin & Healthy Weight Loss Centers" both teach "systems" for losing weight. They don't say, "Hey, try it my way for a couple of days but feel free to add your own new stuff in there as you go along."

In an interview with Krech, she went so far as to say, "Practically any worthwhile weight loss system will work for you . . . if you follow it." In the same sense, you can follow any system taught to you by your upline mentorship (providing, of course, it is proven in that it has worked for others) knowing that, if you follow it faithfully, it will work for you. And following it faithfully means you don't invent your own variation along the way. You stick with it and, if you have doubts or questions, you ask someone upline who is most likely to know the answer.

Keller, Jenks and Papasan, write, "Until you have implemented and worked with a model (a system), you have little business trying to change or improve it . . . strangely enough, against all advice to the contrary, most agents begin by implementing their own ideas and models." The authors believe that, on the contrary, "The best houses and the best businesses get built from clear blueprints, solid foundations, and proven frameworks."

So, regardless of the area in which you desire to succeed, first find a system for doing so, and stay with that system. I suggest resisting the temptation to get too creative, too quickly. Instead, focus on the results. Once you've attained the results, you can then get creative. Of course, once you attain the desired results, you might not want to.

CHAPTER 12

PERCEPTUAL REALITIES

In his book, *Magical Words of the Wizard of Ads: Tools and Techniques For Profitable Persuasion*, Roy H. William relates the oft-told story of the six blind men of Indostan who experienced an elephant from different parts of its body and, naturally, from their individual viewpoints, came to six different conclusions regarding the essence of said pachyderm.

You may have heard this one before. In my opinion, it's quite interesting. The man who felt the broadside proclaimed the elephant to be like a wall. The one feeling the tusk disagreed heartily, opining an elephant to be like a spear. The third, feeling the trunk, thought they were both crazy and said an elephant is obviously like a snake. The other three, of course, from their points of view, had their own opinions.

Williams tells us that, "In perceptual reality, each of the men was correct."

According to the author, "I tell this story because most efforts at human persuasion are little more than one blind man urging another blind man to 'see' the elephant as he does."

What a profound point! It aligns totally with a concept I often find myself discussing in my live presentation, and that is "Belief Systems." In other words, not only do we see the world from our own set of beliefs (all of which were handed to us from family, friends, environment, life experiences, etc.), but we assume everyone else sees the world the same exact way!

Oh, how often I've done that . . . and I'm supposed to know better. After all, I write about this stuff!

But, it doesn't matter. Most of us, more than on just infrequent occasions, slip into this pattern. We know that it's wrong. Unfortunately, we don't remember it's wrong until after the fact, while doing the post-mortem of our presentation in an attempt to figure out why the other person didn't seem to want to do what we wanted him to do.

Have you ever presented your opportunity to someone and, for the very life of you, couldn't figure out why, after explaining to him or her all the incredible benefits of your opportunity and products/services, he or she was no more interested than they were at the beginning of your meeting? In fact, they might have been even *less* interested.

Perhaps . . . ah, just perhaps, you were presenting the benefits that *you* find valuable, exciting and even exhilarating, without knowing whether he or she felt the same way.

"But," you might ask in amazement, "How could she not be taken with the opportunity to travel?" Or, "How could he not be excited by the idea of leading thousands of people toward financial freedom?"

"How could Bill not be totally fired up about getting to own a Mercedes?" What could possibly not turn Anne on about introducing the world to the best health-care products that have ever been invented?"

"Everybody cares about that. I know I do!"

Yes, there's that old belief system coming into play once again. As in, "I think that way, so everyone else does, as well." Or, what my friend, Judi Piani, author of the book, *Trait Secrets: Winning Together When You Don't Think Alike* defines as, "Normal is what I am."

That reminds me of a gentleman I had occasion to meet years ago, shortly after having moved to Florida. He made what I considered to be a rather odd, yet very definitive statement. It went as follows: "Everyone who moves to Florida moves down here either to fish or to boat. Anyone who says anything different is lying."

Hmm, then I must have been lying. Those two activities are just something I've never found to be particularly special for me. Yet, his belief system was so strong in that area that, to him, anyone not having a similar belief, MUST be lying (to themselves, if not to him). After all, as far as he's concerned, "Normal is what I am." I must admit, I generally tend to think the same way of myself.

Now, had he asked me about golf, that would have been different. (Actually, I don't golf either, but it would have been different.)

A lighter (and definitely ridiculous on my part) example is a disagreement I had with someone about 10 years ago. He was thinking about moving to this area and asked if a particular home a Realtor® told him about over the phone was near the ocean. I said, "No, it's pretty far away." So he told the Realtor® he wasn't interested. When he and his wife arrived they asked me to take them to that home just to see it. When we arrived he said, "I thought you told me it wasn't near the ocean!"

ME: It isn't!

HIM: It is, too!

ME: No it isn't!

HIM: Yes, it is!

Let's analyze this: The "truth" is that home was seven miles from the ocean. I, living in Jupiter, Florida and two blocks from the ocean, feel that seven miles is far away. He, being from the Midwest, feels seven HUNDRED miles from the ocean isn't too far away. I'd say our miscommunication had "something" to do with our belief systems. Yes, we are still friends. Why did neither of us think to mention the exact number of miles? I dunno.

Now, let's relate this back to the subject of this chapter. The typical belief system when dealing with a person to whom you are introducing your opportunity (and/or products or services) is to assume that his or her beliefs regarding their goals, dreams, wants, needs, etc. are the same as yours. Well, they might be, but probably are not.

So let's look at an effective way to work with "Beliefs."

During your presentation, ask yourself:

1. How is my personal belief system distorting the way I should be presenting?

2. How is his or her personal belief system different from mine?

3. What questions can I ask this person that will clarify my understanding of their belief system (what they want, what's important to them)?

4. What information can I give that will help them see where my opportunity/product/service meets their needs (not my needs)?

Mr. Williams, mentioned earlier, wrote, "Have you ever paused to consider that your family, your friends, your co-workers, and your customers (and, we could add, your prospects), live in their own private, perceptual realities? Instead of expecting them all to see the elephant as you do, why not try to see what they're seeing? If you're patient, you will finally see enough of the elephant from different perspectives to finally make sense of it all."

"And then", he concludes, "you'll have something to say that will really be worth hearing."

Wow - what a great point!

Suggested practice exercise: for the next month – or forever, if you'd like – be "consciously aware," every second possible, of doing your best to see "the elephant" from the other's point of view. Will it be easy? No, but you'll learn a lot about the other person and their belief system . . . not to mention a lot about yourself, and your belief system; even those things about it which hold you back and keep you from being as effective as you can be.

CHAPTER 13

UNDERSTANDING "THE LAW OF SUCCESSFUL GIVING AND SUCCESSFUL RECEIVING"

(Part 1)
(Excerpted from Endless Referrals: Network Your Everyday Contacts into Sales, by Bob Burg)

As you've seen throughout this book, networking correctly, effectively and profitably has much more to do with giving than it does with receiving . . . at least at first. Through much of what you've done thus far, at this point in the process, you are giving a lot, giving continuously and, especially in the beginning stages of your relationship, it might seem as though you are the only one giving!

Actually, it should seem that way because it's probably true! Not to worry; these actions are currently setting you up for an avalanche of new, highly-qualified prospects for your business and even referrals from those who don't join you. On the product side of your business, the same is true. While we've geared the information in this book primarily to the business-building side, you'll also find that the number of new referrals to potential product buyers (customers) rise dramatically.

Some of those customers, aside from providing additional income for you, will refer you to other customers. And, they might themselves (they and those they refer) eventually become business builders. One never knows.

Networking really is all about giving (being a go-giver as well as a go-getter), and how giving will come back to you many times over. However, there's nothing "la-la" or theoretical about this. It's based on Universal Laws and Principles which have withstood the test of time.

Most people are familiar with the saying, "Give and you shall receive." And, many have seen this happen in their lives. This is the "Law of Cause and Effect." Sometimes this law proves itself almost immediately and other times years later. Sometimes the result comes directly from the cause, and other times indirectly. Some people seem to experience the results of this law more tangibly and in ways easier to understand than do others. But I believe that, intuitively, we all know this law, or principle, works.

The Law of Cause and Effect, in this case, "through giving you receive" (and, typically you end up receiving even more than you give) is a spiritual principle, and like all spiritual principles, has its physical counterpart. In other words, the consistent following of a spiritual principle brings with it a physical manifestation. I want to look at why, when you give, you receive, often even more than you give. That's the major question we'll answer here.

It seems as though our Creator has organized the universe in such a way that every Universal Law has principles that, if understood, embraced, and acted upon, provide results that are predictable over time. If we check into it with enough diligence we can actually explain, through logic, why a principle works as opposed to just saying, "Well, that's the way it is." I believe that was done so that we could tap into an understanding of how the universe works and more effectively work within its laws and principles (whether I'm correct in that belief is another matter; it's simply my personal opinion).

That's important because, as Bob Proctor, one of the world's foremost speakers on the topic of abundance and Universal Laws points out, "If you are successful, but you don't know why you're successful, then you won't know what to correct when things go wrong." Wow! How profound!

One really neat thing about Universal Laws is that they are predictable and consistent. For instance, gravity is not a sometime thing. You cannot step off a ten story building and fall one time, and step off it and float upwards the next time. Universal laws, by their very nature, are consistent. Being so, we are able to tap into certain aspects of our world with certainty. I believe this definitely holds true for the Law of Cause and Effect; in this case, more specifically, giving and receiving.

So, again, why does this Law, or principle, work? Why do we receive so abundantly when we give?

In his book, *The Science of Getting Rich*, written in 1910, the author, Wallace D. Wattles, set down certain rules that, if you follow, will help you to become very prosperous. And, when he talks about being rich, he's talking in terms of financial riches, as opposed to other excellent interpretations and forms of wealth, such as personal fulfillment, happiness, health and so forth. He also makes the point, which I happen to subscribe to, that if you get wealthy the right way, than the other important aspects of your life will be just as healthy as your finances.

One of Mr. Wattles' rules to becoming rich is the following: "Always give more in use value than what you take in cash value." He says, "You cannot give a person more in cash value than you take from them, but you can give them more in use value than the cash value of the thing you take from them."

What does this mean? On one level, the surface level, he means that when you sell a product or service, although you'd go broke if your product or service cost you more than you took in financially, you can, in actuality, provide a product or service that adds to their life more than what they paid for it, while at the same time you make a profit. He describes this in the following manner, in terms of his book which, back in 1910, most likely sold for just a few dollars at most:

"The paper, ink, and other material in this book may not be worth the money you paid for it. But, if the ideas in this book bring you thousands of dollars, you have not been wronged by those who sold it to you. They have given you a great use value for a small cash value."

Excellent point. Of course, I hope you feel the same way about this booklet.

So he was discussing this principle of more use value than the cash value you take from them in terms of a direct sale.

Since, at this very moment, however, we're not talking about the value you're giving due to selling your products or even the value of registering this person as part of your organizational team, but simply in the relationship you're beginning with a new networking partner, let's look at what Mr. Wattles wrote, on still another level.

My interpretation of the saying, "You cannot give a person more in cash value than you take from them, but you can give them more in use value than the cash value of the thing you take from them," can be rephrased and shortened to:

"Give someone more in use value than what you take from them."

This just means to always do your best in adding to their life, to their success, without concern, especially at the beginning, for what you are receiving from the relationship.

There's an excellent reason why, with this type of attitude, you can accomplish much and reach great financial heights. According to Mr. Wattles, "people are built with a desire for *increase* in their lives." When carefully considered, his statement makes perfect sense. After all, since recorded history, human technology has advanced considerably. This, because humans, as an entity, desire increase . . . in their health, wealth, convenience, artistically, spiritually, and in practically every other way imaginable.

This is why, when you have a product, service or skill that can help people increase an aspect of their life they wish to increase, you can make a lot of money. A few quick examples: Percy L. Spencer, the inventor of the microwave oven, satisfied the need of convenience. Debbi Fields, founder of Mrs. Fields' Cookies, tapped into peoples' desire for increase in pleasure, as did a man by the name of Candido "Jacuzzi."

And, there are many, many more on a local level, from the person who helps people satisfy their desire for increased financial security by helping them invest in the right financial growth products, to the computer "troubleshooter" who helps his or her customers satisfy their desire for increase as it pertains to being able to do more work on their computer.

This also means that, at the beginning of a networking relationship, it's beneficial to *impress* the idea upon the other person that, just by being a part of your life, they are bound to find increase; that because of what you provide, whether it's advice, referrals, friendship, information, and more. When people sense that by being associated with you, their life will experience constant increase, they then desire to advance that relationship.

As it happens, this person will typically do so, by doing his or her best to give value back to you.

The following, written by Mr. Wattles near the end of the book is, in my opinion, one of the most profound statements of all time, and is a key to understanding the "way" of the successful networker:

"No matter what your profession, if you can give increase of life to others and make them sensible – meaning aware – of this gift, they will be attracted to you, and you will get rich."

And this leads to one of the most important concepts of all to understand; it's what I call "The Grand Paradox." We'll discuss that in the next chapter.

CHAPTER 14

UNDERSTANDING "THE LAW OF SUCCESSFUL GIVING AND SUCCESSFUL RECEIVING"

(Part 2, "The Grand Paradox")
(Excerpted from Endless Referrals:
Network Your Everyday Contacts into
Sales, by Bob Burg)

In the previous chapter, I mentioned that giving works both from a practical, as well as spiritual side. Let's look now, at just the practical side and see why this works.

Remember, "The Golden Rule" of Networking is, "All things being equal, people will do business with, and refer business to, those people they know, like and trust."

When we give to - or do something for - someone, we take an important step toward causing those "know, like and trust" feelings toward us in that other person. It's often been said that the best way to get business and get referrals is to first give business and give referrals. Why? Because when someone knows you care about them enough to send business their way, they feel good about you.

Actually, they feel *great* about you, and desire to give back to you. They also, simply out of rational self-interest (often referred to as enlightened self-interest) know that you are a good person with whom it's in their best interest to cultivate this mutually beneficial, give and take, win/win relationship.

Of course, it doesn't have to be actual business that you give. It could be information, whether that information is something that would help them in regard to their business, personal, social, or recreational lives, and other areas of interest to them. Perhaps you suggested a book (or bought them that book) that you knew would be of true value to them. Maybe you knew their son or daughter was looking for work at a certain company and, knowing someone there who knew the personnel director, you made a call and put in the kind word that helped ensure employment.

What's important to remember is to give, not with an emotional demand or attachment that the person to whom you gave must give back to you or repay you in-kind, but simply because you enjoy adding to the joy of, and increase in life to, another human being. Give for the right reasons and you benefit greatly. Give for the wrong reasons and you don't.

THE GRAND PARADOX OF
GIVING AND RECEIVING

While you know that giving does in fact lead to receiving, when you give only in order to get, it doesn't work nearly as well. In fact, it has nearly the opposite effect.

Even that spiritual principle has a simple physical explanation: when you give only in order to get, or be repaid, it comes across as such to the other person. You just can't hide it and just can't fake it; at least not for very long. Some people do have a knack of getting away with it for a while more than others, but eventually it will come back to haunt them as well.

No, give because it's something you desire to do, and do it without the expectation of, or attachment to, direct reciprocation and you'll find the giving and receiving aspect of the Law of Cause and Effect to work for you in ways the typical business person will never even imagine.

Thomas Powers, author of the book *Networking for Life*, puts it very nicely: "The energy . . . arises from a willing suspension of self interest." Not the foregoing of self interest but merely the suspension of it. I love that statement by Mr. Powers because it absolutely encapsulates the one trait common to those I call "Superstar Networkers." These people constantly ask themselves how they can add to the life/business of the other person, as opposed to what they can get from them.

Again, though – and this is so important to understand – this does *not* mean they don't expect to prosper. They *know* they'll prosper in a huge way. But they are not "emotionally attached" to having to reap the rewards then and there, or even directly from that person. Thus, they can fully focus on the "giving" part of being a successful networker. They know that the more they give, the more they'll eventually receive. Yes, it really does work that way.

With that in mind, let's see how this principle pertains to those most successful of networkers.

Superstar Networkers

Superstar Networkers; those whose businesses are extremely profitable and personal lives filled with friends and loving relationships pretty much all have two things in common.

Number one, they are givers.

Number two, they are "connectors" of people (which, in a sense, is simply a subset of giving).

Let's discuss "givers."

Actually, first, let's discuss what I *don't* mean by givers.

This is the person who gives only in order to get something back. Or, as the esteemed Dr. Hannibal Lecter so eloquently put it, "Quid pro quo, Clarice . . . quid pro quo." This type of "quasi networker" is typically taken at face value as one who always has an agenda when they do for another.

While this person can and at times does attain his or her share of business, they will never develop the kind of long-lasting, mutually beneficial, give and take relationships with others as will the superstar networkers. They will never elicit the feelings of knowing, liking and trusting from others that typifies the type of networker we all want to – and can – be.

If they do get anything back from the quasi-relationship they just formed, they'll usually only get back (and, often, grudgingly) exactly what they've given - not any more – and most likely from that one source only, and that one time. This is not the case with our superstar networkers.

By the way, what's interesting is that this type of person often thinks that he or she is the ultimate networker. Why? Because that's the mindset and belief system they come from; that networking is a matter of "getting" from others and that, "Hey, sometimes I might even have to give first if that's what it will take to ultimately get what I want from them." Again, though this person will achieve some limited success, it will be merely inches on the yardstick of superstar, profitable networking.

So then, what do I mean by "givers?" Simply this: The superstar, mega-successful, high-dollar earning networker is the greatest and most active giver you know. He or she is constantly referring business to others. He is always on the lookout for a piece of information that will interest someone in his network of friends and prospects (regardless of whether or not it's business related). She is always suggesting ways that someone from whom she purchases goods or services can improve their own business.

They give. They give actively and "without attachment." They are always thinking of what they can give, how they can give, and to whom can they give.

Tim Sanders, author of *Love is the Killer App*, describes this as "the act of intelligently and sensibly sharing your 'intangibles.'" According to Sanders, our intangibles are our knowledge, our network, and our compassion.

Some superstar networkers seem to excel in one type of giving above and beyond any other, and become known for this. For example, always recommending great books, or constantly making introductions to people who can benefit one another. Mike Litman, author of *Conversations With Millionaires*, talks about how this creates what he calls, an "asset of value."

This is what you "bring to the table" in your relationships with others. And, it doesn't cost you a cent! (Or, perhaps the price of a book, stamp, or time on the Internet.) The result is an appreciation of you by that person. Mike has even given this concept a name; he calls it "loverage." That's where you use love and leverage to help others help you. Of course, to do that, you are first helping them – in Mike's case, through your particular asset of value.

What's interesting is that successful, giving, profitable, superstar networkers seem to have a "knack" for hooking up with other success givers. Yet, it's not luck. They look specifically to identify these types of people. Why? Because they know that while average networking relationships are 50/50, the most exciting and profitable ones are 100/100.

In other words, both people are trying so hard to help the other person succeed, that success comes back to each of them in spades.

These same people are also what are called "connectors." They are always asking themselves who they can set up with each other. They know that everyone they know and/or meet might be a valuable contact to someone else in their network. The fun part is introducing them and setting up the relationship.

You can probably see how the goodwill and positive feelings you're eliciting in others can come back to you in incredible abundance.

A True Networking Superstar

A perfect example of this is my friend, Bea Salabi. While she is not a Network Marketing professional, her example is one which we can all model.

Bea, who owns a local mortgage lending company, came into town a relatively short while ago. At the time, it was just she and her former business partner. Bea is the prototype of the successful giver. A year later, Bea had three very profitable offices and over 30 team members. A huge success story.

Bea is a person who goes out of her way for anyone and everyone she can, from sponsoring a family of eight children, to serving on her local board of directors for Habitat for Humanity, to taking over 1500 local underprivileged children to the movies in one summer. And, please don't think she does this with the idea of acquiring business. She doesn't (although, "oddly enough," it always seems to happen).

On the other hand, she also throws huge, lavish parties for her prospects and clients. From this, she knows she'll eventually receive business, and she really goes all out in providing food, a massage therapist, and many other goodies. Though this is part of her business public relations efforts, she's just the type that when she gives, she goes all out. It's part of her very nature. What I've found is that very seldom does one successfully have a business personality and a separate non-business personality. Bea certainly proves this true, as she gives whether it's simply for charity or for business.

But, here's a typical Bea story of how giving, just for the sake of giving, leads to receiving many times over. And this is just one example. A woman was getting her home foreclosed upon. A couple found out about it through their church – the same church as attended by the woman – and came to Bea, saying they'd like to buy the house to prevent the foreclosure. They would hang onto the home, they said, until the woman was able to buy it back from them.

This being the case, Bea offered her services for free. She did not receive one cent from that transaction. However, as a result of her giving efforts, she received numerous referrals resulting in – now get this – over 25 closed transactions, for which she did in fact earn commissions. How? Apparently, the couple, who turned out to be true "centers of influence," felt that Bea's efforts should not go unrewarded, and they began spreading the word about her. This is what happens to successful givers.

Be like Bea, and all the other ultra successful networkers (such as those in your upline of mentorship) who know that the way to receive in abundance is to be a giver and connector, and to do so with the main goal being to genuinely help the other people in your network. Do this consistently, and keep adding people to your network, and you'll be like a waterpump that's been correctly and sufficiently primed, and receive a steady, gushing flow of referrals.

CHAPTER 15

IF NETWORK MARKETING IS A GAME, HOW DO YOU KNOW WHEN YOU'VE WON?

I was recently asked that question and my first answer was, "It's not a game, it's a business. It's a big business."

But, the person asked again.

This time I responded, "It's not a game, it's a system of distribution."

But, he still wasn't satisfied and said, "C'mon, Burg, you know what I mean. You, more than anyone, make everything into a game, so answer the question, 'If Network Marketing is a game, how do you know when you've won?'"

Okay, I decided to play along. And, voila, it now becomes the final chapter in this book because I believe that – by answering this question – we get to see what Network Marketing is truly about.

So, here it goes:

In order to effectively answer this question, it might be a good idea to first define the three major elements of the question; "Networking", "Game" and "Won."

The reason is that since all of us come from our own world view or paradigm and with our own personal definitions of each term, an answer without definition might lead us to agree or disagree without knowing exactly why.

Networking. (Burg's definition): "The cultivating of mutually beneficial, give and take, win/win relationships." By its very definition, this means there can be no losers.

Game: One dictionary definition says, "An activity providing entertainment or amusement; a pastime." Like a professional athlete who loves their sport like the game it is, but still approaches it as a business, the same might go for you. Hopefully, you're having fun while you work; you enjoy the challenge, the learning, and the people with whom you work. And, while you don't necessarily like everything about the game of Networking, you at least – as Jim Rohn used to say – "appreciate the opportunity it provides you."

Won (Win): According to Webster's, "To succeed or prevail in an effort. To triumph, to be victorious."

But, if you prevail or triumph, does that mean someone else has to lose? Well, since, by the very definition of Networking there cannot be a loser, the answer is no.

Then, over whom do you triumph?

If you must triumph over someone, perhaps it is yourself. It's getting past your fears and reaching out in order to sow the seeds of a new win/win relationship; to cultivate that relationship, and even to do the things necessary to reap from that relationship, and then being able to duplicate those results by helping others.

But, how do you know when you've won?

If Networking is a game, you know you've won if . . .

- You feel really good about the relationships you're cultivating.

- The people with whom you are cultivating these relationships feel really good about the relationship you're cultivating.

- You find your prospect list getting bigger and bigger, with higher quality people.

- You are adding increase, wealth, prosperity and happiness to the lives of others.

- You're getting to present your business and products to more people than ever before.

- You've reached a higher achievement level within your company.

- You're on your way to reaching a higher achievement level within your company.

- People seem to gravitate toward you in ways they previously did not.

- Your check is getting bigger and bigger.

Are the above happening in your life and business? Is success on the outside beginning to manifest? If so, it's a direct result of your personal growth on the inside.

And, if you're continually growing on the inside . . . then you KNOW you've won the game!

ABOUT BOB BURG

A former television personality and top-producing sales-person, Bob Burg speaks to corporations and organizations worldwide on topics at the core of The Art of Persuasion. Addressing audiences ranging from sixty to sixteen thousand, Bob has shared the platform with some of today's top business leaders, broadcast personalities, coaches, athletes and political leaders, including a former U.S. president. Bob is also coauthor of the Wall Street Journal best-seller The Go-Giver, Go-Givers Sell More, and It's Not About You. His classic copies and is still used today as a training manual in many corporations.

For more information on Bob's resources and speaking availability, visit www.Burg.com

PROSPECTING NOTES

PROSPECTING NOTES

PROSPECTING NOTES

PROSPECTING NOTES

PROSPECTING NOTES

PROSPECTING NOTES

PROSPECTING NOTES

PROSPECTING NOTES

PROSPECTING NOTES

PROSPECTING NOTES